D1441206

Daughters of Dakota

Stories of Friendship Between Settlers
and
the Dakota Indians

edited by
Sally Roesch Wagner

with
Vic Runnels

Victar H. Runnels

Volume 3

GFWC of SD/DOD
Box 349
Yankton, SD 57078

*To Joybelle —
In Friendship & Reconciliation —
Sally*

The cover illustration by Lakota artist Vic Runnels was commissioned for this book and illustrates the stories of friendship that developed in the early days of Dakota settlement.

The photographs, chosen by LaVera Rose, are from the Pioneer Daughters collection of the General Federation of Women's Clubs of South Dakota. The collection is housed in the South Dakota Historical Society.

DAUGHTERS OF DAKOTA
P.O. Box 349
Yankton, SD 57078

To my mother,
Lorraine Aldrich Roesch
pioneer daughter
1911-1990
in the spirit of reconciliation

TABLE OF CONTENTS

ACKNOWLEDGMENTS

As I write, I am surrounded by envelopes with my name written in my mother's distinctive handwriting. They are filled with newspaper clippings which kept me posted on all the Reconciliation events that were happening in South Dakota during the 100th anniversary of the massacre at Wounded Knee. When she and my dad moved back to the state last year, my mom began saving every related story from my hometown paper, the *Aberdeen American News.* Each time I'd see her, she'd give me a new batch of information. Such was her support of my work.

In amongst the clippings I find a press release on one of her activities, dated May 1, 1990, which reads:

Mayor Tim Rich of Aberdeen today accepted a gift of Reconciliation on behalf of the city. "Charging Hawk," an original water color by Aberdeen artist Vic Runnels, was given to the city by the descendants of Alva N. Aldrich, who served as mayor of Aberdeen from 1904-1910 and again from 1916-1921, in honor of his years of public service.

"My father was a great believer in ethnic pride and diversity," said Lorraine Aldrich Roesch, daughter of mayor Aldrich. "The family has been wanting to do something in Dad Aldrich's memory, and this seemed to be the right time, with the Governor declaring this the Year of Reconciliation. We feel very fortunate to have a noted Indian artist in our community doing this picture for us."

Vic Runnels, whose work is known internationally, said, "A majority of my themes, and especially my water colors, are related to dreams and visions. Men went out to fast and pray, and had dreams and visions that suggested names. A lot of my paintings suggest family names, as this one does." He went on to say, "I appreciate the chance, in this Year of Reconciliation, of hopefully creating a better understanding of Lakota people and Lakota culture."

It was one of my mother's last public acts; two months later she died of injuries received in a car accident.

When I moved back to South Dakota to be with my dad after my mom's death, Vic and I began to research and write together, and to become friends. It is this friendship between the granddaughter of an Aberdeen mayor and the nephew of a man who carried an injury from the Wounded Knee massacre, that gives me hope that we in this state can begin to heal the wound created by my people.

Vic agreed to work with me on this manuscript as an editor, and he sculpted it as an artist: sketching the bold strokes of direction and flow and then filling in the details with explanatory footnotes and contextual knowledge. It was a pleasure to work with him, and I am grateful for his steady hand in the project. The mistakes that remain are mine.

Thanks to La Vera Rose, Tillie Black Bear, Mike Roberts, Arlene Beuchler, the Swanigans and the staff at Pine Hill Press for help in getting the book out.

Finally, my mother's spirit permeates all my work. She raised me up with a knowledge of my heritage and taught me to respect it.

PREFACE
by Virginia Driving Hawk Sneve

"At first people were afraid of the Indians but they soon learned that the color of their skin and hair did not make the person," recalled Betsy Himle Swenumson as quoted by Sally Roesch Wagner along with the recollections of other *Daughters of Dakota*. Betsy's and the other stories included here, gives a view of the relationship of white women and Indian women rarely glimpsed in Dakota history.

As Betsy and the editor noted, fear of the Indians was common among the whites. Long after the Sioux Uprising of 1862, they were afraid that they would suffer the fate of the white settlers in Minnesota. Hysterical rumors fed the fear, and the white women tell of how they hid their children and other treasures or fled in terror, only to find the Indian scare are false. These recollections show that this irrational fear was slow to die, and some white women developed a life long distrust of Indians. But others came to understand that their fear was based on ignorance, and after they came to know individual Indians, the fear and distrust was replaced with pity, compassion, and in some cases, friendship.

Sally Roesch Wagner doesn't editorialize on the misunderstandings, but lets the reader judge through the words of the white women. These recollections present the ambience of the period when the word "squaw" was frequently heard, and the Indians did not protest the derogatory offensive meaning of the term.

Also included in this volume are stories of mixed-blood women whose dual heritage and allegiance, bicultural understanding and bilingual skills enabled them to bridge racial and cultural differences. They, and some full-blood Indian women, showed in their stories how they were able to overcome cultural upheaval and adapt to reservation life.

In many of the stories white women tell how they taught Indian women to sew the cloth which replaced tanned hides, to cook new foods, and to keep a house in place of a tipi. Other tales relate how the Indians taught them to find and prepare edible plants and berries as food or medicine. Thus, the white women learned that the Indians reciprocated kindly deeds with friendship.

No matter the race, all of the women in this book were determinedly adaptable to the rigors of a new life whether it was in a homestead shanty on Dakota plains or on an Indian reservation. This third volume of *Daughters of Dakota* gives insight to the past which enriches the present.

Virginia Driving Hawk Sneve

INTRODUCTION

This is half a book. The stories are of exchange, the interaction between two very different groups of women: the Dakota* and the white women who came to settle on their land. But the stories are all told from the non-Indian woman's perspective.

Because this is a preliminary, or working manuscript, it will be issued in a limited printing, to be followed by a complete book which contains both Indian and pioneer women's stories of their interactions, including accounts of the massacre at Wounded Knee in 1890.

There is a reason for the one-sidedness of this book. Drawn from the Pioneer Daughters collection of almost 6,000 stories gathered over a forty year period by the General Federation of Women's Clubs of South Dakota, it is the third in a series of six volumes which will explore the scope of the collection. While this single focus limits, it also yields some important new insights. As the story of white women on the plains is only beginning to be told, these accounts can add to our emerging knowledge.

We learn here of the discrepancy between the almost pathological fear of Indians the pioneer women absorbed from their culture and the unexpected friendship and close proximity with Indians which they found when they arrived in South Dakota.

These interactions were not smooth, rather they were characterized by cultural misunderstandings that cut both ways. While Indian protocol, belief and practice were hard for white women to fathom, the world-view of a people who preached that it was more blessed to give than receive, but didn't offer the whole loaf of bread must have been equally confusing to the far more generous Native Americans.

Despite the differences, cooperation and coexistence developed. Pioneer women often were alone on the prairie, and their fear came face to face with the open-the-door-and-walk-in policy practiced by those they so desperately feared.

Given massive cultural differences and the absence of a common language, compounded by deep prejudice and fear, it's amazing that friendships and understanding could ever bridge that cultural chasm.

On the Indian side there is a generosity of spirit transcending injustice that makes my heart ache as I, a pioneer daughter, go through these stories.

Not satisfied with the land the Dakota leaders with great thought and care agreed to make legally available for white settlement,** my people went beyond the boundaries and took illegally what had not been offered them. The injustices compounded, piling one on the other.

The pioneers seemed unaware that Washington was failing to pay the bill for the land, the rations and annuities upon which the Indians now depended for survival. The settlers faulted the Native Americans for "begging," demanding or taking the food which was rightfully theirs.

The surprise is not that the Indians fought to maintain stewardship of their land; the wonder is that there was so little bloodshed. It was the remarkable restraint demonstrated, ironically, by the "fierce, war-like Sioux" in the face of spirit-breaking provocation, that kept the prairies from going up in smoke.

As my Lakota colleague, Vic Runnels (Ishnala Wecha), says, "the wonder is not that some of us survived, the wonder is that any of us did, with all the genocidal policies against us. I think that has something to say about us as a people."

*Called the "Sioux" in a majority of history books, the word comes from the Chippewa, "Nadewisou," which means "treacherous snake." Our actual name is Dakota (or Lakota or Nakota in the other two dialects), which means "allies" or "the people". [V.R.]
**I think these leaders really wanted peace. They worked so hard to maintain it, despite bad agents and bad government policies. [V.R.]

THE AUNGIE FAMILY
early settlers

DESCENDANTS OF COL. ROBERT DICKSON
He was known to the Chippewas as Shappa (The Beaver); Dakota term, Capa. He died in Queenstown, Ontario [in] 1823.

Children:
Robert Dickson m. sister of Red Thunder (Chief of the Cut Head Yanktonais). Her name was Ista Toto. [Green Eyes, V.R.]

Mary Dickson m. Henry Aungie. Henry Aungie was a nephew of Wabasha, a chief of the Sisseton-Wahpeton band of the Santee Sioux tribe.

CHILDREN OF MARY DICKSON & HENRY AUNGIE
Victoria Brazeau
Harriet Aungie
Mary Van Metre Aungie
[Matilda Aungie Lyman]
[Thomas Aungie]

Harriet Aungie; Clay County, 1890
Harriet I. Aungie was of the third generation of descendants of Col. Robert Dickson, a British army officer who was the representative among the Indians of Canada, in 1890, of the government of England and his duties in that capacity took him on frequent occasions into the peninsula of Michigan.

Col. Dickson was a Scotch Presbyterian. He married a native Indian woman of the Yankton tribe, which tribe at the time roved through Wisconsin and Lake Superior and around Lake Michigan.

Rev. A. N. Coe, an Indian Presbyterian minister who is also employed as an interpreter in the United States Court of this state, in speaking of his deceased aunt a few days ago said: "It seems that Col. Dickson, though he lived on

1

the frontier and led the life of a pioneer, endeavored to bring up his children in the faith in which he had been reared, that of the Presbyterian church, which accounts for the fact that his descendants, even his great grandchildren, are members of the same church.

"After the war of 1812, Col. Dickson became a citizen of the United States and was employed by the American Fur Company and had his headquarters at Lake Traverse, in Minnesota." Col. Dickson sometime in the 1830's died at Niagara Falls.

"His son, William Dickson and Henry Aungie, who became a member of the Dickson family, marrying the daughter of old Col. Dickson, followed the fur trading business and those two men in selecting a point from which to operate, founded Fort Vermillion, on the Missouri River, where the present town of Vermillion, Clay County, stands.

Later they were located at Ft. George, which was south of Ft. Pierre of the present day, and it was at Ft. George that Harriet Aungie was born to Henry Aungie and the daughter of Col. Dickson, who was herself a half breed. October 28, 1841, was the date of her birth."

"Though they were engaged in fur trading on the Missouri River, these Indians went to Minnesota to receive their annuities from the government and as schools were few in those days and Henry Aungie wanted to educate his daughter Harriet, he placed her in a mission school at Lac Qui Parle, [sic] Minnesota, which school was in charge of Dr. T. S. Williamson and Dr. Stephen I. Riggs, the latter of whom was the father of Rev. A. L. Riggs, who founded the school at Santee agency, and after whom the Riggs Institute is named.

"Harriet was placed in the mission home of Rev. Robert Hopkins and it was there, as a girl, that she saw the impressive scenes which were connected with the signing of the great treaty of 1851, by which the land in eastern Minnesota was ceded to the whites.

"In her fourteenth year, Harriet Aungie received an injury from which she never fully recovered and was wheeled about in a chair the remainder of her life.

"After the signing of the treaty of 1851, Henry Aungie located on a piece of land east of Sioux City, Iowa, in the

Lloyd River Valley and some trouble which occurred at that place between the French and the white settlers of that neighborhood was known and is still referred to as the Aungie war. Harriet witnessed that trouble."

"Harriet possessed an excellent memory and she never forgot the teachings of old Major Dickson and his wife, who were devout Christian people, and after leaving the vicinity of Sioux City, in 1875, and going to live on the Yankton Reservation in Dakota, she and her sister, Victoria Aungie Brazeau, organized the Dakota Native Women's Missionary society, which is in existence today. Through their influence as missionary workers, several scores of Indian women were converted to Christianity.

"Their brother, Thomas Aungie, who had also gone to the Yankton Reservation from Sioux City, was an elder in the Presbyterian church at Greenwood for a quarter of a century and during all of that time was a member of the Board of Home Missions of the Dakota Presbytery and also organized the Young Men's Christian Association among the Indians of Dakota.

"It was through her influence that I entered the Presbyterian ministry government position which I hold now and to which I expect some day to return.

"Harriet I. Aungie's mind remained clear to the last moment of her life and she died, leaving an impress upon the circles in which she moved, among her people, which time will not efface.

"Rev. John P. Williamson, who pioneered with Dr. Stephen Riggs, in preaching her funeral sermon, paid a brilliant tribute to the memory of the humble Indian woman who had done so much good in her quiet effective way."

Mathilda Aungie Lyman; Tripp County, n.d.

Mrs. Lyman is the Aungie baby who figures in the story of the "Aungie War" on the banks of the Floyd. In the year of Sioux City's beginning, there was an organization known as the claim club, the object of which was piously proclaiming to be the protection of each other's rights and claims. The right, however, which they were protecting was a questionable one, namely the claiming, under the pre-emption, of 320 acres instead of the legal 160.

A part-blood Frenchman named Henry Aungie, who had been in the employ of the American Fur Company on the upper river, had married the daughter of Col. Robert Dickson and his Yankton Sioux wife. In 1854 Henry Aungie decided to make his home near the mouth of the Perry Creek, and the Sioux and the Floyd Rivers. He camped for a while near the Travercier home at the time the Townsleys were neighbors of the Traverciers and had with them, as boarders, Hiram Nelson and Rufus Rowe.

The story goes that Rowe fell in love with Victoria Aungie and asked her father to bring his family to live in the log house which he was building on the east bank of the Floyd opposite the present site of the Martens and Ketels mill. The tradition in the Aungie family is that Rowe spent more and more time with the Aungie family and that, when Aungie had the house built, came and lived with them. The family also denies that Victoria gave him any serious encouragement, as she had a sweetheart among her own people. Rowe became ill with a serious malady that affected his mind and after he was taken away from Sioux City for care, he died. Land in Sioux City by that time was eagerly taken. When it was learned that Rowe was dead, others began plans to get possession of his claim.

The question was at once raised whether the claim belonged to Aungie or to Rowe. Had Rowe lived he and the Frenchman would no doubt have arrived at a satisfactory settlement. With his death occurring under such circumstances and with the claim being considered desirable by the promoters of the town, trouble was inevitable. The story was circulated that Rowe had been given poison by a friend of the Aungie's, an Indian girl, We Washita, which had first made death – [threats] so that the Rowe family might have the claim. This story is not given credence by those who knew the Aungie family though it was used to justify the claim club in its rather severe course.

The claim club served notice on Aungie that he was requested to get out. Aungie asserted the right to the land and proposed to stay there. He was in possession and was living on the land. He seemed to have every right to stay. It must be remembered that at that time Sioux City was many weary miles from any seat of government and the claim club was its own law. Aungie was given a day or two to get out or the claim club would drive him out. Aungie refused and when he had told the other French men, who were living on the big Sioux and below the Floyd, they rallied to help Aungie hold his claim.

The given day arrived and found all the Frenchmen waiting at the Aungie establishment. Aungie did not think that the claim club would come. He thought its' request to be absurd for the members to insist that it be carried out. The tension at the little house across the Floyd was great that morning as they waited for the attack which was not made. At last it was noon.

"There," said Aungie, "They did not come. I did not think they would."

The Frenchmen cautioned him that the day was only half done; but Aungie refused to think that the threats would be carried out. He announced his intention of going to work at his plowing, saying that he had lost enough time. His assurances affected the Frenchmen until they began to think that he was right. They decided to go over to the town to see how matters progressed. Whether they were tricked into drinking at Sangster's store or whether they all collected voluntarily is one of the disputed points in the story, but they did go to Sangster's store and they did all have several drinks and they did wake up to find themselves prisoners in the store.

In the meantime Victoria Aungie, known to the pioneers as "Prairie Flower," looked from the door and saw a group of men approaching the Floyd ford in a wagon and armed with axes and guns. She gave alarm and her father came running from his work in the field. He ordered the family to get out of the house and run toward the timber on the bluff. He took his gun and leveled it toward the invaders. His wife clung to his gun and begged him to put it up and to make a peaceable settlement. He declared that there was no settlement to be made—that he would shoot the first man who touched his house to tear it down as the claim club had threatened. He made Victoria and the rest of the children hide themselves out of danger. His wife, the daughter of Col. Dickson, refused to go. Harriet, the crippled daughter, sat crying with the baby in her arms.

The men approached the house. They came near enough so that the family inside could hear their voices and something brushing against the side of the house. Mrs. Aungie clung to her husband begging him not to shoot. The waiting became unbearable. Aungie by accident or because his nerves could no longer stand the delay, fired his gun into the floor. The shot was answered from the outside, splintering the wood and sending bits into the faces of the baby and Harriet. Mrs. Aungie screamed.

Then came a knocking at the door, Aungie answered it. It was Goulet, a Frenchman from Sioux Point; he asked Aungie to open it. He said the claim club wanted to talk to him and that Goulet had given word that no harm was to come to Aungie if he would come out. At first Aungie refused. His wife insisted. They opened the door. The men of the claim club were anxious to make peace. The thing had gone farther than they had intended. They had expected Aungie to recognize their authority, the authority of power; and to meekly bow to their decree. His position was fast crowding them into a course which would mean trouble which might bring investigation that they did not care to have. They offered to buy Aungie out. He refused. They coaxed. He was silent. They asked him to name a price. He said his claim was not for sale. They collected $100 in gold and offered it to him. Mrs. Aungie begged him to take it and to give up the claim. Still he refused. Someone thrust the gold into her hand and Mrs. Aungie gave them her assurance that they would go away. The men considered her answer final. Perhaps they were glad to get off so easily.

When the claim club had recrossed the river Mrs. Aungie had persuaded her husband that standing their ground would not be worth the danger nor the unpleasantness and they gave up their claim to go farther up the river. Of these sisters none are now living except the baby Matilda, who makes her home in Greenwood. Victoria, "The Prairie Flower" married among her own people, having had, according to her sister, no other intention. [From *Sioux City Journal,* 30 May 1926, by Gertrude Henderson.]

Clara Lyman Uken; Yankton County, 1888

Clara Uken's grandfather, William Penn Lyman, the man for whom Lyman County was named, was the first white man to build a home for his family in Yankton County. He had been with General Harney's troops in the Nebraska campaigns. There he married a full blooded Yankton Sioux woman and, in 1857 with his wife and family, he came down the Missouri River to settle near the mouth of the James River. There he built a home for his family and established a ferry.

Major Lyman was a leader among the early settlers of Yankton and the surrounding area. This is illustrated by his rescue of the new agent Burleigh and $30,000 worth of annuity goods for the Ponca agency from the grounded river boat, and by the fact that it was Major Lyman who led a squad of reconnoitering cavalry in the vicinity of Yankton during that frightening year of 1862, when the inhabitants of the city were living for a time within the stockade. It was also Major Lyman who was chosen to head a delegation of emissaries to Strike-the-Ree. Thus he is credited with the fact that "old Strike's" group of hostile young tribesmen by-passed Yankton in that fateful year.

Mrs. Clara Uken's father, Max Lyman, was born in 1846. After his father's death he accepted the responsibility for guiding and educating his younger brothers and sisters. Max Lyman spent most of his youth in Yankton in the days of Todd and Jayne and in his later life was the issue clerk at Greenwood, that most beautiful of the South Dakota agencies. This was where Clara Uken was born.

Max Lyman married Matilda Michelle Aungie, Clara's mother, at Springfield in 1881. Matilda Aungie was the granddaughter of Col. and Mrs. Robert Dickson. Matilda's grandmother was a sister of Red Thunder, the chief of the Cut Head Yanktonais. Col. Dickson, a famous Scottish born Canadian fur trader had been rewarded for his services with the British forces during the war of 1812, with the rank of Colonel.

Matilda Michelle, a Yankton Sioux, was born at Sioux Point, in 1856. She had been orphaned when she came, with one brother and five sisters, to be near the Rev. John P. Williamson family, in Yankton in 1869. The Aungie family had known the Williamson family in Minnesota so these sons and daughters of old friends sought protection from the

Clara Lyman Uken (Sioux Indian)—1888
Yankton

Williamsons after the passing of Aungie's parents. Matilda was frequently a member of the Williamson household, until her marriage to Max Lyman.

Clara Uken was one of the eight children born to this union. She was born in 1888. She vividly recalls life at that agency in those early years; going aboard the steam boats that still plied the river; visits to their home by those 1860 pioneers; once a visit by the sister of J. B. S. Todd, South Dakota's territorial representative to the Congress of the United States.

Mrs. Uken attended the Alfred Riggs Normal Training School at Santee but refused a scholarship to a higher institution of learning in order to assist her mother in the care of a bedridden aunt, Harriet Aungie. Although Harriet was physically helpless for fifty-seven of her seventy years, she was a brilliant woman who had considerable influence on early legislation pertaining to South Dakota.

Clara Lyman acted not only as her nurse by also as her secretary, writing for her letters to Commissioner Burke and members of the Congress, helping often to affix Harriet's notary seal to those letters. Part of that correspondence and beside discussions with local and national leaders of that day were instrumental in bringing about the passage of the law which sanctioned the sale of Indian heirship land; later Harriet sold her land.

Harriet also assisted Rev. Williamson by teaching an adult Sunday School Class. This class was held at her bedside.

Among Mrs. Uken's many memories is that of Portas B. Weare of Sioux City. For him her Aunt Harriet beaded a complete costume of Sioux regalia and, when Mr. Weare returned from the Klondike gold rush, he brought Harriet gold nuggets.

Mrs. Uken's Uncle, Henry Lyman, was the first Indian ever to be graduated from Yale. He became a lawyer but died soon after graduation.

A cousin of Mrs. Uken's, Mrs. Jane Waldron, was the first Indian to ever bring a law suit against the United State's Government. The suit, which she won, was over land on the Cheyenne and involved an Indian named Tin Cup.

Mrs. Uken was baptized by the Reverend Joseph W. Cook, an early Episcopalian missionary, and confirmed by

Bishop Hare at his Cathedral of the Holy Family in Greenwood.

In 1914, Clara Lyman married Otto Uken, who passed away in 1958. To them were born four children.

Mrs. Uken, in July of this past summer, did not know her grandmother Lyman's heritage. She learned later that her name had been "Winona." Your letter was the first knowledge she has had that Strike-the-Ree was an ancestor [of this full blood Yankton Sioux woman.] [Rev. Cook was at Wounded Knee, treated the wounded after the massacre. Many firsts here to investigate further–S.R.W. and V.R.]

Jane Elizabeth Van Meter Waldron; Clay County, 1861

Her father, Arthur Charles Van Meter, had run off from his home at Martinsburg, Virginia, when only fourteen. He got as far west as Dakota Territory and joined up with General Harney's forces and was with them when they made their trip in to the Black Hills in 1855; he also spent the harrowing winter with those troops at Fort Pierre. He settled at Vermillion and there met and married Harriet Aungie who was the granddaughter of Col. Robert Dickson (officer and liaison for the British about 1812) and his Indian wife. In Harriet Aungie was mixed the blood of her two paternal grandfathers, Scottish from Col. Dickson, and French from the Aungie side, and native Indian from her grandmother.

There were five children in the Van Meter family. Mr. Van Meter prospered in that early frontier town, and was liked and respected for his generosity to those less fortunate, while indulging his children in proportion to his means. He was always in sympathy with progress and was one of the moving spirits in erecting the "Old Log School House." Jane later became the first president of the Old Log School House Organization, founded in 1901. Jane early showed a desire for learning, and attended school throughout what the early school had to offer.

When Jane was about eight years old, the Bower family moved to Vermillion, and on first sight Jane Van Meter and Alice Bower became childhood friends–"best friends." A deep and lasting friendship was maintained through the long lives of each of them.

Alice, who wanted to be a journalist, was hampered in her first attempt to work in a printing office by certain paternal views, but was bolstered in her ambition by the support of A. C. Van Meter who said, "If Cal Bower won't let his daughter work alone where only men are working, I'll let my daughter work with her," which was what happened. Alice, at fourteen and Jane at thirteen, went to work learning to set type at the Vermillion *Plain Talk*. Alice Bower Gossage went on through life as a printer, a writer, and finally joint owner with her husband, Joseph Gossage, of the Rapid City *Daily Journal*, to become the beloved "A. G." whose column was a timely forum for every conceivable interest in the pioneer town of Rapid City, and in the long years achieved state and nation-wide recognition.

Jane, meanwhile, had her ambition – to go to college. On funds she earned she enrolled at Bodon College in Wisconsin, and was happy there for the short time circumstances permitted her to remain. However, with what proved throughout her life to be so characteristic, she yielded to the call of duty and returned home because of an emergency which developed to be only temporary but also proved to be the end of her college. It was indicative of the reliance her whole family had on her, and family came first. No doubt her father could have ably afforded to send her through, but at that time girls didn't go to college, and others in the family couldn't see what she wanted to go for, or what good it would do her. It was the one deep regret of her life.

Her love for learning continued the rest of her lifetime. She had a remarkable memory and read widely with the result that she was a very accurately informed person, and was recognized as such by all in the respect and reliance accorded her when dates, facts, authors, etc., were under question. Her strength combined with judgment was of that nature that in family matters others depended on Jane, and later her position with her own family was that of the rock in times of stress. No misfortune or untoward incident could prevail against her fortitude and optimism.

During the seventies when the government was paying bounty on the buffalo, and while vast herds still roamed the midwestern plains, Arthur Van Meter, with his venturesome nature, equipped with all the essentials for the

hunt, took his entire family and some other of his wife's
relatives, and set out to hunt buffalo for bounty. Jane was
about 16 at the time. Their following of the herds took them
west through Dakota into Wyoming and Montana. It was
a dangerous business, but strangely that phase never seemed
to effect them. The only incident which caused alarm was
the approach of a party of Crow Indians, and great apprehen-
sion was felt until the Crows showed themselves to be friendly.
The trip was of further interest in that Viola, the eldest,
was married and this was their honeymoon trip. Over two
hundred of these kingly beasts fell to their guns. To kill
a buffalo even with present day high-powered guns is no
easy matter for a novice, so one can measure the skill required in maneuvering the approach to an alert herd and
getting set, for the big buffalo gun had to be supported
by a stationary device and time was needed for the aiming
and firing.

One of the guns used on this adventure is still in the
possession of one of Jane's sons, George Waldron. As usual,
in those times, people were wont to profit where it was possible
in order to add to needed articles. With foresight, Mrs. Van
Meter and the girls cut the heavy curly hair from the
foreheads of the animals for use in mattresses. One is still
in use after these 75 years, and the vitality of that hair
is such that it still has the life and springiness of new hair.
It is one of nature's greatest protectors of the buffalo for
it is said that the bullet from a high-powered game rifle
cannot penetrate its mass, and that a buffalo hunter never
tries for the kill in the forehead.

The family returned to Vermillion for yet a few years.
But once again Jane—at about seventeen—left the home circle on an ambitious mission. Taking the steamboat which
plied between St. Louis and Bismarck, she got off at Ft.
Pierre. Her idea was to teach school. Her accomplishments
in that regard while not what would be deemed requisite
for latter day standards were enough better than most in
her environment to make her services in demand.

She let it be known, and speaking both English and
Indian fluently, she was sought by Peter Dupree, a Frenchman married to an Indian woman who desired his children
to be educated. She readily accepted and spent a winter

in their home on the Cheyenne Reservation. The town of Dupree is named for this fine man. He also it was who initiated the present herd of buffalo in the South Dakota State Park, although it is doubtful if he could had seen that far into the future. One spring after a buffalo hunt, five calves were left orphaned, and he took care of them until a sizeable herd was built up. Later either he or his estate sold the entire herd to James (Scotty) Philip in 1905, who put them under fence on land leased from the government. The foresight of these two South Dakotans made possible the preservation of this great kind of the plains.

Following this year's experience, Jane returned to Ft. Pierre where she was chosen to teach by a group of parents to provide schooling for their children. The pay was fifty cents a month for each child. Many of the students were older than she. The pupils included members of the Hearst family, the George D. Matherson and LaPlante families and many others. It was during this time that she met her future husband — Charles Westbrook Waldron. Mr. Waldron was one of the legislators elected to the Territorial Legislature. Their stay here was short for it was still a very new town, and in hostile Indian country. The Waldrons, who had always maintained friendly relations with the local Indians, nevertheless felt it necessary to leave when the Government troops from nearby Yankton moved all the families over to Yankton. One family had been massacred by the Indians, filling the others with alarm.

The family resided in Yankton about twenty years when they, too, made the journey up the Missouri to Ft. Pierre. Here Mr. Waldron practiced his profession and the son, Charles, established himself as a freighter between the Missouri River and the Black Hills, operating the then ordinary mode of transport — bull teams. On one such trip, which was a matter of six weeks, he brought in to the Black Hills the first steam boilers for the Homestake Mine.

Jane Van Meter and Charles Waldron were married in Ft. Pierre June 30, 1885, and set up housekeeping in a very small, two-room house, located on 640 acres of land joining Ft. Pierre immediately on the north; this land had been allotted to Jane Van Meter by the government because of her Indian inheritance.

Changing conditions led the young couple to abandon the freighting, and so they invested what means they possessed in a small herd of cattle. It was Jane's idea. The business of selling his horses demanded that much of the time Charles was away from home, both in the seasonal round-up of the stock, and absences to see them. Jane was aided only by a hired hand who had been left in charge of the ranch. She enjoyed the responsibility, and met the many and varied instances of early day ranching with the common enough pioneer spirit which took all in its stride.

There was the time when out riding the trap line she discovered a large grey wolf dead in the trap. Riding a favorite horse "Roany" she was unable to lift the animal to the horse's back, so decided to "snake" – or drag – the wolf at a rope's length tied to the saddle horn. Either the horse was not yet broken to such duty, or the scent of the wolf frightened him, and he bolted with Jane in the saddle – the wolf wildly flopping at the end of that lariat while he tore, terror stricken, for the ranch. Roany, while a pet with the Waldron children, all of his long life, could never be induced to draw anything on a rope length. Psychiatrists would have an easy explanation for that mental quirk now; it was just as readily understandable then.

Another time the hired man came in with the news that "Teddy," a very small Shetland stallion who never seemed to sense the difference in his size and that of the large stallions, had in a battle with one such, gotten a kick which broke one of his hind legs. The hired man was all for shooting him. "No," said Jane, and taking the stone-boat (a triangular contraption made of two logs boarded over, on which barrels of water were hauled) Teddy was ignominiously brought home, where with their combined efforts he was pulled up in a rope-sling by Jane and the hired man, and Jane set the leg. Teddy ever after walked with a slight limp, like horses with a knocked-down hip, but his valor remained.

In the hard, unseasonable blizzard of May 5, 1905, stockmen suffered terrible losses; great herds of cattle, horses, and sheep were nearly wiped out, and of those remaining, thieves made off with many more. The idea, from the viewpoint of a thief, was good and most timely, for following that blizzard spring riders found it impossible to determine whether stock was stolen or frozen. Teddy was, however, undoubtedly among those driven off to Canada, for his little carcass was never found amid the piles of dead horses on his range.

There was that time when Charles, having gone to Ft. Pierre for supplies, was delayed in returning by a hard snow and spell of cold weather. The larder had gotten alarmingly low when one morning – lo! and behold – the family cat brought as her offering to the door step a small rabbit. Had she sensed the need? It was a more than timely event and that day the family ate well on tender rabbit.

The children were reaching school age and although Jane had already taught them to read and write, it was decided to move near a school. One winter was spent at Forest City, then the family moved back to Ft. Pierre.

Jane was happy to be again among people, she was a gregarious soul. When the cause of woman's suffrage was foremost with many South Dakota women, she joined their forces and was the State Corresponding Secretary of their organization, and active in the work of securing the franchise for women. She was appointed by Governor Andrew Lee to the various state institutions – the penitentiary at Sioux Falls, the mental hospital at Yankton, the school for feeble-minded at Redfield, the training school at Plankinton. She served long and creditably in this capacity, and was reappointed by several successive state administrations.

Jane did a nice business in giving local dances which were popular with the Pierre and Ft. Pierre patrons alike. There were the regular dances with local musicians providing the music, and with a spirit of enterprise she imported "name" groups to play which was more than remunerative. It was in that period just preceding the advent of motion pictures, and the dances were quite the social events on the various holidays.

MISSIONARIES AND MILITARY

Philena Everetts Johnson; Sully County, 1867

Near or in the year 1867 Colonel Irvine, who was at that time Commander of Fort Sully, brought her to the Fort from Keokuk, Iowa to be a Governess to his children, one of these children being Louise Irvine, who later married Thomas L. Riggs and became a missionary to the Indians. Miss Everetts stayed on at Fort Sully after the army troops stationed there had organized a school, and continued to teach there.

She had come to the Fort by steam boat, that being the only means of transportation in that day – these steam boats sometimes came from St. Louis, sometimes from Yankton and ran to Fort Benton, Montana, that being the only means of transportation to this great unsettled part of the great Northwest.

Miss Everetts was a cultured, refined woman and very well educated, being a college graduate, an unusual thing in that day. She taught the children the usual grammar school subjects of that day, but music and French and Latin, as well. When her pupils went to eastern colleges they had little trouble with the college entrance examination. We do know that Mrs. Riggs, who was at that time Louisa Irvine, went to Oberlin College, one of the better colleges in Ohio.

Phile Everetts married Eli Johnson, who had been holding down a claim at Calliope, which was probably a Post Office in some claim shack in Sully county. They came to Highmore where they established their home and where they lived out their lives.

She was a member of the first Women's Investigation Board, being appointed by Governor Mellette, first Governor of the State. Prominent in Woman's Christian Temperance Union work, having been one of the state officers, she was for years one of the officers of the Women's Suffrage movement. In fact, it was while working in Pierre in the interest of this organization that she contracted the cold which led to her death.

16

Louisa M. Riggs; Sully County, 1867

It was her father-in-law, the Rev. Stephan Riggs, the pioneer missionary, who in 1840 conducted at the nearby Fort Pierre, the first Protestant service in the territory. Her husband, Dr. Thomas L. Riggs, soon after graduating from Beloit College, began in 1872 the first Protestant mission in this part of the state—located across the river from Old Fort Sully. Soon after, he opened the first missionary day schools here and over the reservation for the Teton Sioux. There the Indians were taught to read their own language.

In 1876 materials were freighted by steamboat from Yankton to build the little white chapel, the first church in this area. It is still in good condition, the only one left of the old mission buildings.

In 1885 Mrs. Riggs helped to organize the first Indian boarding school where only English was taught. In this school the industrial arts were emphasized to help raise the standard of living among the Indians. The work was not all done in the school, but Mrs. Riggs drove with her husband by horse and buggy over the expansive prairies stopping at the tents and lodges to show these primitive people the white man's way of doing things, caring for the sick, for the papooses* and teaching the mothers how to handle household problems.

It was right here on Peoria Bottom—so called because the old steamboat, "Peoria Bell," carrying supplies to Fort Sully, was grounded—that Dr. Riggs introduced irrigation and taught the Indians how to raise vegetables for year-round use.

Dr. Riggs was even in on the last buffalo hunt that took place in 1880. He had been invited by Lazy White Bull, nephew of Sitting Bull. Too, it was this missionary of whom it might be said closed the era of Sitting Bull himself. For it was he who with some Indian friends, two weeks after the death of this Hunkpapa chief in 1890 went to his abandoned camp and buried the frozen bodies of the Indians that lay just as they had fallen in the battle—the dead included Crow Foot, the chief's own son. Few, perhaps, understood the Indians and worked with them as smoothly as did Dr. and Mrs. Riggs.

Mrs. Riggs, too, had ample opportunity to know them, for 84 years of her life was spent right in this area. It was in 1868, at the age of nine that her father, Major Irvine,

Louisa Irvine Riggs
Autumn of 1880

came to Fort Sully which at that time was the only white settlement between Yankton and Bismarck. At the time when Yellow Hawk and his tribe occupied Peoria Bottom and Sitting Bull was wielding a great influence with all the Dakotas. At the conclusion of her schooling in the East, this cultured, well-educated lady began teaching in the day school in this wilderness mission. The school had little in common with the schools of today. Although they taught reading and writing, their biggest task was to teach the Indian family how to live according to the teachings of Christ, and to give them advice on matrimonial problems for at that time the Sioux were polygamous, and several wives under one tepee at times caused trouble. Pretty hard for a man like Dr. Riggs, even, to convince them that one wife was sufficient.

Up until 1913, the boarding school was a hive of activity with the Indian children learning to do things with their hands – learning to live as well as to read. Mrs. Riggs' musical education was a great help. She not only gave music lessons, but played for church up until a few years ago. Her grand piano, which must have been an object of admiration, was in constant use.

These missionaries also witnessed the opening of this section to homesteaders, and it was Dr. Riggs who intervened on behalf of the Indians so that those who had occupied the land would get the first chance to file on it.

In 1989 the original mission house was destroyed by fire and all their treasures burned. It was then that the large mission house was built on prairie round heads, the work done almost entirely by Dr. Riggs and his devoted Indian friends.

It is at this house that Mrs. Riggs spent her declining years, Dr. Riggs having died in 1940. Here Indian friends were always welcome. At times one might find several tepees pitched in the yard – for the Indian usually carries his tepee with him. To them she was the symbol of the great spirit and inspiration. [By Ida B. Alseth in Sioux Falls *Argus-Leader*]

... The site was known to the Indians as Ti Tanka Ohe, the place of the large house, the council houses built by the Ree Indians. It was also called Peoria Bottom after the "Peoria Bell," one of the steam boats that plied the river, went aground nearby. Oahe is the corrupted form of Ohe. Whites couldn't get the sound without inserting a vowel.

Oahe was the site of much missionary work with the Indians. There was a boarding school, an industrial school, the chapel for worship, always the stone house in which everyone was welcome.

Over the fireplace in the living room is a dedication, its message is one reason persons do not forget the stone house at Oahe:

"We dedicate this place to sacred hospitality — together we take a vow — to turn no man or woman from the door, to see no friend maligned, no foe betrayed, within these walls, the walls of our dear home. It shall not be a home in a little sense, mere selfish shelter for two mated folk but it shall be a home for all who knock. And he who eats our salt here in our tent we shall leal to, even tho he sin." ["leal" is a poetic form of "loyal." From unidentified newspaper clip.]

*Algonquin is a term meaning baby or newborn.

Sarah Van Nuys Williamson; Brule County, 1866

In the spring of 1865 a meeting of the Minnesota Presbytery was held in Winnebago. Rev. John P. Williamson was a member of the Presbytery but for two years he had been with a band of 1300 Santee Indians at Ft. Thompson, Dakota Territory, where they had been banished after the outbreak of 1862 in Minnesota. Anxious to attend the meeting he left for Winnebago, going down the Missouri River by row boat to Yankton and from there by stage and on foot to Winnebago. He arrived in time for the meeting and was entertained in the Van Nuys home. Here Mr. Williamson met Sarah and in the week he stayed at the house the acquaintance ripened into a friendship and by correspondence later into a betrothal. The date of the wedding was set for April, 1866.

Again Mr. Williamson set out from Ft. Thompson for Winnebago, traveling again by boat, stage and on foot. The going was arduous, since all the creeks and rivers were running bank-full due to the melting snows and on the day set for the wedding, Williamson was unable to arrive at the Van Nuys' home in time for the hour set for the ceremony. The assembled guests, and especially Sarah, were much relieved when he arrived, however in no shape for a marriage ceremony. However, it took place. Mr. Williamson and his bride at St. Paul embarked on a notable honeymoon trip, which took them down the Mississippi River on a steam boat to St. Louis and finally on another boat coming up the Missouri to Niobrara, Nebraska.

The next summer Mr. Williamson and the Indians moved two miles down to Bazille Creek, where he erected a three room log house, the large middle room being used for services as well as a school room.

That fall the Williamsons were joined by Edward Pond and bride, both of whom Mr. Williamson knew well in Minnesota. Now life took on a more pleasant aspect. It was here that Winifred, their first child, was born. After two years the Indians were again moved, some twelve miles down the river to a permanent location, and the Santee Agency was established across the river from Springfield, Dakota Territory. Here Mr. Williamson began the creation of a permanent mission, erecting a church building, residence, and a school which later became the Santee Normal Training School, which under Dr. A. L. Riggs became a great influence for good among the whole Sioux Nation.

Mrs. Williamson, meanwhile, was doing what she could in precept and example to further her husband's work. She was mistress of a Christian household where the Indians came in numbers for help and instruction and incidentally, to view the operations of a Christian home. This example had good effect, as it was not long until a considerable number of the Indian homes took on a neater aspect and where the Bible was read and prayers offered every day.

In 1869 Mr. Williamson moved to Greenwood and opened up mission work among the Yankton Indians. This tribe had no missionary and little contact with the whites, and were wild and much given to superstition and idol worship. On the 18th of March, Mr. and Mrs. Williamson, with two small children, Winifred and Guy, crossed the river to the Yankton Agency.

Mrs. Williamson was by this time somewhat inured to the life of a pioneer missionary's wife. Reverend Joseph W. Cook, of the Episcopal Church, opened a mission at the Agency the following year and the two missionaries labored side

by side in their efforts to bring the heathen aborigines out
of their pagan worship and practices into the light of Christian living and civilization. Notwithstanding, for a number
of years the nights were made hideous with the incessant
beating of the drums at the war and grass dances, and the
shouts and shrieks of the participants.

In the meantime, the family was enlarged until there
were eight children, four boys and four girls.

The old grandmothers of the tribe were frequent visitors
to the kitchen, where they would sit on the floor and talk
and complain more often to themselves than to anyone else
until they were given something to eat. In the work of the
mission, her help, especially with the women, was a great
aid. She was instrumental in organizing the Women's Society of the church and served as treasurer of the Society for
forty years.

Ethel Collins Jacobsen; Hughes County, 1883

Ethel Collins came to Oahe, South Dakota with her
parents in a covered wagon from Washington County, Iowa,
when she was twelve years old, arriving at Oahe Mission
on October 12, 1883.

After attending school at Oahe mission, where she and
her brother and sister had English classes under the teacher
for the Indian children, she was sent to an aunt in Keokuk
to go to high school and later went to Multon, Missouri
to the Synodical college for women.

Her father's sister, Mary C. Collins, had come to Oahe
as a missionary to the Dakota Indian in 1875, and later
went to a mission station of Grand River on the Standing
Rock Reservation (now the village of Little Eagle) and made
her home there until 1910. During her summer vacation her
niece, the subject of this sketch, spent two or three months
with this aunt and after her return from school in Missouri,
taught for two winters at the Oahe Mission Boarding School
in 1890.

She recalls that she went to Blunt to take the teacher's
examination, and to her dismay found herself not only con-
siderably excited and alarmed over the prospect but also
with an attack of laryngitis which made it impossible for

her to speak above a whisper all day. The county superintendent at the time was Corsby G. Davis and she was very appreciative of his kindly consideration and was gratified to receive a second grade certificate, no higher being granted to a first time applicant.

Her experience with the Indians and her aunt's life work among them had made her plan to be a missionary also but as in other similar cases, marriage changed her plans. She became engaged to Elias Jacobsen, a young man who, after graduating from Beloit College, came to Oahe at the same time the Collins family arrived and was associated with the Rev. Thomas L. Riggs at the school there for a number of years, later becoming its superintendent.

Ethel Collins' mother died in the fall of 1891, leaving four young children, besides three who were grown. Having the contract to teach the Little Eagle Indian Day School that winter, with a cottage for the teacher at her disposal, she persuaded her father to bring the children and spend the winter in it with her, the two older children being away at school. Until school closed in the early summer following, she kept house for the family, taught the Indian pupils English, reading, writing, and arithmetic, and helped with the mission services in the native language, which she had learned to some extent on Sunday, visited the sick when her aunt was absent, and lived a busy life.

Her father remarried that fall, and in 1891 she and Elias Jacobsen were married by the Rev. George Reed, missionary at Standing Rock Agency, the ceremony being held in the log mission school room chapel.

They set up housekeeping at Oahe, about a quarter of a mile from the Mission in a house of hewn logs that had been built on a site about a mile away and later moved. The building was one put up by General Harney who had established an Agency there in 1868.

The Jacobsens moved to Pierre in 1896, and the log house was moved again about four miles farther down the bottom. The first child Edmund was born in this house, which served as their residence and a small general store as well as the Oahe postoffice.

After they came to Pierre, four other children were born. She became a reporter on the staff of the *Pierre Dakotah.*

She opposed the woman suffrage movement. This was not because of any idea of women's inferiority, nor because she thought that they might not actually have the right to vote, but because she felt that their duties were different from that of men; that they were not sufficiently devoting themselves to their own peculiar fields and as she says now, from a sort of blind fear that unless something be done to stop the ever increasing desire of opportunity for women to make the care of their children and homes secondary to their interests, juvenile delinquency would increase and the security of the home be endangered. Men, she said, could not share the responsibilities of women in these matters as women might share men's political and business interest. Of course her fight, for she accepted the position of secretary to the South Dakota Anti-Suffrage Association and spoke and wrote for some time against the movement, was eventually lost. She was literally persecuted for her stand, but says to this day that she does not regret it, nor feel that women show they have gained and not lost for themselves and their children, by winning the ballot. She has, however, always voted as a duty.

Addie Jordan Williamson; Sully County, 1883
When Addie and [her sister] Ethel finished the eighth grade, they took teacher's examination and taught in rural schools. There were no high schools that early. Addie was fortunate in having a chance to teach in a school three miles from Onida. She could drive home from there. She received $27.50 a month wages. Addie also attended Pierre University, now Huron University.

Rev. Jesse P. Williamson came to Onida for his first pastorate. He was the grandson of Rev. Thomas E. Williamson, the first Protestant minister in Minnesota and the son of Rev. John P. Williamson who came to Dakota Territory as a missionary to the Indians in 1863.

He was born at Greenwood March 10, 1872. He was a graduate of Yankton College and Princeton Seminary. He and Addie were married on June 19, 1900.

The Yankton Agency, about 60 miles up the river from Yankton, was where J. P.'s father was stationed. In fact, he had started this mission. Here the four sons were raised.

There were also four girls in the family. Their Post Office was Greenwood.

J. P. served the pastorate in Onida and Blunt from November 7, 1897 to March 25, 1909, then took up pastorate work in Charles Mix County from October, 1911 to November, 1913. Addie had joined the Presbyterian Church and was a true helper all the way through. Of course she didn't teach after she was married because married women did not teach in the early days. She had taught for two years before her marriage.

The Santee Indian Normal Training School was located across the river from Springfield. Dr. Riggs was in charge. This was a Congregational school. In 1913 this denomination wished to have the help of the Presbyterians. They wished them to furnish a man and his salary and money for building.

Mr. Riggs worked hard to get J. P. to come to fill the place and finally persuaded him to come. He had charge of evangelistic work. They were there for five years. Mr. Williamson, of course, moved his family there. He was Sunday School Superintendent, held evening services in English and mid-week services. One reason Mr. Williamson was so valuable was because he could speak Indian.

Two hundred people took a Bible Correspondence Course. The task of correcting the papers fell to him. He had an assistant in an old Indian preacher. He was here for five years. His father died and left his work so J. P. went to Greenwood and after a short time he was appointed to take the work of his father and was Superintendent of all Presbyterian missions among the Sioux, in North and South Dakota, Minnesota and Montana. There were seven Missions in the Sisseton Agency alone. He continued his work for eight years. His health was not good enough to keep on longer.

The board offered him a years leave of absence but he did not accept and went back to Onida to live. He was pastor here again at the Onida Presbyterian Church. He was here for ten years when he retired at retiring age. Yankton conferred on him the D.D. degree in 1934. He had been Register of Deeds from 1887 to 1893 and now after his retirement, he was elected Clerk of Courts from 1937 to 1939.

During the first World War, [Addie] again taught school. She volunteered her services because of the shortage of teachers. There were twelve children in the neighborhood where they lived and no school. These were white children so she worked through the County Superintendent of Schools and a carpenter and had a new school house built.

She won the confidence of the big boys who had been expelled from the Greenwood School twice through Divine Guidance and good Child Psychology and the school was a success in every way. She then taught in Greenwood.

In 1932, when the Onida band did not have a snare drummer, she played snare drum. She had always wanted to play drums and since both her children played and knew of the shortage in the drum section she had the pleasure of being with the young people in the municipal band. They wore white so she sent and got her a nurses uniform so she would also be dressed in white.

When the Union Circle which was an auxiliary of the Community Church was organized, in Onida, Mrs. Williamson was the first President and we find in the History of Sully County that when the Old Settlers were organized, Addie Jordan had charge of the music.

Mrs. Williamson lists as the unpleasant experiences of her life "The Blizzard of 1888," "The Indian Scare of 1890" and the "Prairie Fire of April 2nd, 1889."

An account of "The Indian Scare" is also written up by Mr. Jordan in the Sully County History. He says in part:

In the controversy over signing a treaty with the Indians in regard to opening a tract of land between the White and Cheyenne Rivers – this was Sioux land – the commission had met with considerable opposition. Several Sully county people were there among them with Mr. Jordan.

Conditions became very tense and Big Foot's Band of Indians started for camp. The tom-toms kept Mr. Jordan and Mr. Kimmel awake all night where they were trying to sleep on the opposite side of the river. In the morning there was another conference and then the issue was left to the Indians.

The tense feeling among the Indians was, in a measure, responsible for the ghost Dance Craze which followed. The white settlers reading about this got so excited that when Sitting Bull was killed and some Indians started across the reservation to join their friends on the Rosebud [she mistakes

Pine Ridge and Rosebud – V.R.] the report started that the Indians were on the war path and killing settlers in Sully County. The men of Onida got together to plan how they would protect the women and children. They invited them all to a home on the hill where the Indians could be seen if they came toward the house. It was a small five room house and crowded. When Mr. Jordan told Mrs. Jordan, she dressed in her Sunday clothes and called the girls and had them dress in their best.

She wrapped the most prized possessions in a red table cloth, among these were the family albums. The women felt perfectly safe on this beautiful October moonlight night because they knew that the men had guns with which to protect them but what they didn't know was that the guns were twelve gauge and the ammunition was ten gauge. These had been borrowed from the sons of Veterans Organizations and by mistake the ammunition didn't fit the guns.

By morning it was conceded that there was no outbreak and they were glad that the scare was over with no worse results than the heart attack which one woman had. The *Chicago Inter Ocean* paper came to Blunt daily. The Indian scare was written up as well as an article about a family ill with scarlet fever. The article said that this family was brought from the country and housed in the livery stable. This story was untrue because two bachelors had given up their home for the victims of scarlet fever. The folks in Chicago wrote for their loved ones to leave this God forsaken country. [By Averil Amsden Ross, from visits with Mrs. Williamson and from the Sully County History.]

Ann Harris Lang; Yankton County, 1873

As there were few doctors in that pioneer country there was a great need for nurses. In 1873 during the regime of Reverend Joseph W. Cook, she was associated in the work among the Indians at the Mission of the Holy Festival at Yankton Agency.

BOSS FARMERS AND BLACKSMITHS

["The wonder is that, in spite of all this, we have remained Lakota." V.R.]

Coraline E. Saxton Boesl; Bennett County, 1893

Coraline E. Saxton—named after Cora Saxton McKinley, wife of the President and who was either her Aunt, sister of her father or his cousin—was born in Hillsdale, Michigan, the first daughter of John and Mary Saxton, on May 15, 1870. After the death of her father, when "Cora" was fourteen, she came west with her mother, four teen-aged brothers and a small sister. The family had planned to come before, but the father's illness and death intervened, so that the trip was postponed until 1884. They came in a covered wagon and drove oxen.

The family immediately filed on a homestead at Whitney, Nebraska. That same year, their stock all died from drinking alkali water on the place. The discouraged family then took another claim fourteen miles west of Crawford, Nebraska and close to Fort Robinson, Nebraska. At that time, this Fort was the only active station in the west, and from here, the soldiers and officers attempted to quell the numerous uprisings among the Sioux Indians. Chief Sitting Bull and Chief Crazy Horse were most active and most belligerent during this period.

John J. Boesl—colorfully known as "Zither Dick"—was a teamster at the Fort, also the musician for all the affairs and functions for miles around. He and his zither were inseparable and the music which came from that little German instrument was heavenly.

Cora met the musician while attending a dancing party at the Fort and they were married August 28, 1887, when she was seventeen. They had a military wedding, solemnized by Father C. T. Clevers, in the Episcopal Church at the Fort. Cora was exceedingly calm during the ceremony, then abruptly spying the faces of some negro troopers, looking

28

in from the outside, thru the windows, her composure vanish-
ed. Their witnesses were Colonel I. Fletcher and Best Man,
Lieutenant B. S. Humphrey. Mr. B. S. Paddock, who ran
the Post Trading Store at the time, presented the young
couple with a complete set of furniture.

They immediately took a homestead and after experienc-
ing all the trials that went with such a venture in those
times, "proved up" and that same farm, by the way, is still
in our family.

Five children were born and my father was away much
of the time taking part in Indian skirmishes. He kissed the
oldest little girl, Teresa, goodbye on one such occasion and
when he returned home, found that she had died of black
diphtheria. They lost the three oldest children.

Then, in the year of 1893, they came to the Pine Ridge,
my father as "Boss Farmer," when Cora was twenty-three.
By this time, she was not the sheltered, timid girl from
the east, but had matured into a courageous pioneer. However,
the savage Sioux Indians were still resenting the "Whites"
and it was with no little amount of trepidation that she
faced her new experiences.

The Indians were still without Christian names or
clothing – her first job was to help her husband to name
and clothe the Indians. To this day, there is a predomination
of the names of the Disciples and Biblical women among
the Pine Ridge Indians. Each person was ushered into the
office by the Indian policeman; my father handed him his
name – Matthew, Peter or Paul, and my mother gave out
with Ruth, Mary or Rachel. They were then given their shirts
and trousers and yards and yards of bright calico to make
dresses.

Cora taught them to sew, taught them not to cook the
government issued soup, but to cook the beans and use the
flour to make squaw bread. She taught them how to roast
and grind the green coffee and how to use the sugar. Up
until this time, the flour sacks were slit and two men on
horses, each holding a corner of the hundred pound sack,
went whooping across the prairie, jubilantly scattering the
white flour.

The government issued cattle to be killed for beef, and
this always called for a gala hunt with bows and arrows – to

kill the cattle. The Boss Farmer had a slaughter house built to eliminate killing the beef in this way and behold, one night a group of the outlawing ring-leaders burned it to the ground. This was the most frightening night of any.

Shortly before this act of hostility – Cora looked out the door when she heard a loud wailing, and there, coming toward the house on horseback, were an aged man and woman, gashes cut in their legs and arms, and covered with blood. They were mourning over the death of a grandchild. What did Cora do? She talked to them as best she could, went to their camp and brought in the little dead child. She got a canned tomato box, which she covered for a coffin and had the first Christian burial on the Pine Ridge. Previously the corpse was tied securely to a piece of board, and placed in the high branches of a tree. The old Grandparents were named "Two Crows."

The night the warriors rebelled and burned the white men's slaughter house, this same "Two Crows" stalked up to the house, laid his hand on Cora's head and with these words, "No harm shall come to one of these fair hairs," he laid himself across the door and spent the night, guarding his friend.

The rebellious Chiefs were rounded up and made to rebuild the slaughter house, which naturally caused a great deal of bitterness. Almost at their wits end to cope with the situation, the couple thought of a plan. They had noticed on the Almanac, that on a certain date, the moon would eclipse – so all the leaders were invited to come and just as the eclipse appeared, our father drew his six shooter and pointing toward the moon, shot. Then when it cleared slightly, he shot again and from then on he was considered as having "magic." There was no more rebellion.

Christmas was unknown, so when the Yuletime approached, Cora decorated the office with a Christmas Tree and the Boss Farmer was to be Santa. All the Sioux timidly assembled, with wonderment and joy over the tree; but the moment Santa appeared in red suit and homemade mask – all that could be realized was Pandemonium. Indians were climbing out the windows and running out the doors, tragically scared of the "Spirit." What a let down after all the work and preparation.

In 1896, the family moved to Allen, which in 1913 became a part of what is now Bennett County. Here, Cora continued her unselfish labors, acting as nurse, doctor and undertaker. She drove many many tiresome miles in the buggy and the team, old "Sam and Turk," doctoring, delivering, and teaching. "Old Sugar" did the housework and each fall the children were sent away to school, to return in the spring. The years passed by and with the coming of the government doctor, there came also the huge half-gallon bottles of castor oil, laudanum and salts—which lined one wall of the office and which was given out on the doctor's recommendation.

One time a family came to get Cora to "lay out" the old grandma, who had passed away in her chair. They had neglected to come, however, for several hours, so that grandma's body was still in the sitting position and rigor mortis had set in. We fail to recall the solution to this problem.

We heard only the humor, the light part—never the loneliness and fear which must have stalked her existence. Her life was simply a dedication to the Indian people—but in 1922, her tired heart gave out and she left us at the age of fifty-two, a symbol of brotherly love—if ever there was such a one. She lies beside our father in the Indian Cemetery north of Allen, still spoken of with reverence and love by the Indian people. Her monument—Unselfishness! [By two of her daughters: Mabel O. West and Myrtle P. Wordeman]

Anna M. Hanson Lein; Brule County, 1883

Anne Margaret Hanson was born in Kvikne, Norway, July 12, 1853. She immigrated to America in 1880 and found employment first as a laundress in a hotel at Mitchell.

About this time her husband was transferred to Lower Brule as a boss farmer and here their second son was born making him the first white child to be born in what became Lyman County.

Mr. Lien was among the first to leave when the Great Lower Brule Reservation was opened to filings on February 11, 1890. He squatted on Medicine Creek and what is now Earling Township, Lyman County.

When he had a one room, two story log house partially enclosed, he went and brought Mrs. Lien and now four children to their new home.

Hardly had they become settled when a cyclone came and unroofed the house lifting the baby boy out of his second story crib to the ground safely depositing him under a log that was left tilted enough for protection. Their home being centrally located and more spacious than any other they made it available for church and Sunday School as well as any other public meeting.

One night after retiring an Indian uprising was heralded and a band of six Indian braves knocked for admittance from a driving rain.

Not knowing their intent and not wanting to anger them they dared not turn them away. Needless to say she slept not a wink as the Indians stretched themselves on the floor near their bed in every available spot to sleep.

Lizzie Elliot Holmes; Charles Mix County, 1882

In 1891 they moved to the Lower Brule Indian Agency then located about two miles west of the town of Oacoma, where he entered the employ of the government as Agency blacksmith at the wage of $90.00 per month, a sum almost unheard of at that time. Mrs. Holmes was fearful of living among the Indians, as the Wounded Knee massacre was still fresh in everyone's memory, and a company of soldiers was camped along the river to assure peace among the Indians when the Holmes family arrived in Lower Brule Agency.

The Indian women, greatly interested in the doings of white people would peer in at the windows which would be suddenly darkened by an Indian squaw* with shawl outspread to shut out the light, and they would stare into the room unabashed, for minutes at a time. Harry Holmes, husband of Lizzie, with two half-breed helpers soon learned the Dakota language and became quite proficient in the use of it. His Indian name, "Mázajagà" (meaning Iron Worker) was used by all the Indians when the Holmes' arrived in Lower Brule.

Grace Howard, an Episcopal Missionary, came out from New York and worked among the Indians. Coming from a wealthy home, she was much better dressed than the government employees, but her escapades did not help the work of the Indian Mission. Rev. Luke Walker and his white wife, Sophie, served the little Episcopal church at the Agency. Harry Holmes filed on a piece of land across the American Creek in the spring of 1893 and moved his family into a log house vacated by Indians. The Lower Brule Indian Agency was moved to the present site. This log house had white sheeting tacked over the rafters and a good coat of whitewash made it become quite habitable. He opened a blacksmith shop in the little village of Oacama which was then called Gladstone. The Federal Government decided to discontinue the Lower Brule Agency and moved it north to Little Bend where it was operated in connection with Crow Creek Agency on the east side of the Missouri River. All buildings were either moved or sold. The largest residence, called the Major's House, was moved to Oacoma where it was remodeled. It had been the location where the Black Hills treaty between the Sioux Indians and the U.S. Government was signed. [By Mrs. John B. Wart, daughter.]

[*The term "squaw" was widely used by these early settlers, apparently with no knowledge of its insulting and obscene meaning. In these more enlightened times the term is no longer used. —S.R.W.]
*I have not changed this word, because I have not changed words anywhere in the text. However, the term is extremely derogatory and offensive, and I maintain it in the manuscript with mixed feelings.

Jessie Craven; Shannon County, [1895]

With the announcement that she has engaged a manager for the Open Buckle ranch west of Wanblee, 94-year-old Mrs. Jessie Craven will . . . take it easy for the first time since she was married in 1881. She is small and quiet, with great poise and dignity, but whatever had to be done, she could do, and in emergencies she has even helped out at branding time.

Mrs. Craven's lifetime on the Open Buckle ranch includes experiences that might have come from a history book or a Western novel.

The most famous and dramatic story about her had its origin when she was teaching Indian school shortly after the Wounded Knee trouble. The father of one of her pupils was angry when she kept his daughter after school and came to take the child home forcibly. When she couldn't dissuade him, Mrs. Craven, knowing that she must preserve her authority at all costs, called for the agency policeman. This so enraged the Indian that he shoved her out the door and pulled out his knife to stab her.

Mrs. Craven has never lacked for spirit and determination. She grabbed the braids of each side of the Indian's head and had clawed him severely before the policeman came to take charge and rescue, not Mrs. Craven, but the Indian. It is characteristic of Mrs. Craven that after the excitement had calmed down she settled the matter for which she had kept the Indian girl after school and then she herself took the girl home. This story amuses Mrs. Craven as much as it impresses the listener.

Craven was appointed boss farmer for the Indians of the agency and with Mrs. Craven teaching the school it was natural that all officials and supervisors from the Indian service in Washington should headquarter with them. There were other visitors. Theodore Roosevelt, later to be president of the United States, stayed with them a week in about 1885 to explore the Badlands and observe the progress being made with the Indians. He visited Mrs. Craven's school and with characteristic vigor joined the Indian children in singing "The Star-Spangled Banner."

It was she who planned the Christmas party for all the Indian families in the region. The first year she had the children decorate the school house and they got a big cedar for a Christmas tree. In the absence of conventional trimmings they decorated the tree with flowers made of several layers of bright flannel cut in petals and blanket-stitched.

The busy children had not been told that their behavior would bring them gifts of shoes and clothing collected for them by Herbert Welch of the Indian Service.

Some time before, Welch had visited the school in company with Theodore Roosevelt and other officials, and had been deeply impressed by the conduct of the little pupils. They were industrious and obedient as they went through their tasks at the tap of a bell.

Welch was especially impressed when the little dark-eyed pupils, joined by Mr. Roosevelt with his characteristic gusto, sang "America" with a childish fervor although their parents had only recently been at war with the whites. Mrs. Craven loved to teach the Indian children, finding them eager and cooperative, and that day justified all their young teacher's pride in them. That was why Herbert Welch sent out several boxes of shoes and clothes for the Christmas party.

Craven, then boss farmer at Kyle and later the founder of the well-known Open Buckle ranch, was Santa Claus at the party. Mrs. Craven still laughs as she recalls how he looked in his light brown fur coat stuffed with pillows and his big beard made of cotton. The Indians knew nothing about Santa Claus or Christmas and the white man's feast day was a new and possibly alarming experience for them.

As Mr. Craven, outlandishly garbed and repeating the Sioux word for "grandchildren" in an unnatural voice, came into the schoolhouse to distribute the oranges and sacks of candy and the clothing, a wide-eyed squaw [sic] suddenly wailed the Sioux equivalent of "What is this coming!" and slumpled to the floor in mortal fright.

With the exception of that one incident, the first Christmas party at the Kyle Indian school was a great success.

As she taught and kept house and entertained, Mrs. Craven also brought up her seven children.

After the death of her husband she took over management of the ranch and all who have had dealings with her say she has a keen and steady head for business. The ranch has flourished under her guidance. [Adapted editorially from three newspaper articles in the Pioneer Daughters collection by Joy Keve Hauk, two of them not identified, the third, published in the *Rapid City Daily Journal* on 2 August 1959.]

Ann Aurilla Mac Daniels Johnson; Custer County, 1883
Their decision to come west to make their permanent home brought them to the Black Hills via wagon train, although they had stopped in Springfield, South Dakota, near an Indian reservation, where he was employed by the

government and, while he was engaged in his work, she proceeded to teach Indian children even if it meant bringing them into her own home which was later enlarged to accommodate all.

As a young bride she was terrified of the Indians although their trip west was uneventful in this respect. After their arrival, the Indians did steal their team and saddle horse. In telling me about this she told me how she was trying to make the first batch of bread she had ever attempted and upon hearing a noise near the door she turned to see three Indian squaws [sic] watching her and that she almost froze with fear but noticing their friendly looks and their out stretched hands she forced herself to smile, beckoning them to come into her kitchen, which they did, and proceeded to teach her how to make bread. From that day until she died she excelled in her bread making. Later, due to this friendly gesture on her part, she and grandfather found their horses had been returned and were tied in the back yard, none the worse for wear. Grandmother taught these squaws [sic] and others many of our ways, including quilt making. Her children acquired many of the Indian ways associating and playing with their children, even learning to speak the Sioux language.

They were blessed with fifteen children, four who died in infancy in my Grandmother's arms of whooping cough and diphtheria. My Grandfather made their tiny caskets which my Grandmother tenderly lined with sheets and they buried their babies on the ranch with their own simple rites.

Florence De Bell Youngquist; Todd 1885

When I was only three months old we moved to Omaha Indian Agency, Nebraska, where my father was Government Doctor and sub-agent. Then in 1885 he bought a store at Rosebud Agency, Dakota Territory, and also practiced medicine there for twenty-three years.

When I think back and remember how peaceful and pleasant conditions always were and know that it had been only twelve years since the Custer Battle, it seems marvelous that the Indian people could settle down and be so friendly and peaceable in so short a time.

Even at the time of the Ghost-Dance/Wounded Knee trouble in the winter of 1890-91, some of our Indians went to the Badlands to join the hostiles but the ones who remained were very quiet and friendly. The 9th Cavalry were camped around us all winter, but many of the Indians told us they would protect us if any trouble came. We were fortunate in having fine English gentlemen as agents and they took great pride in getting the Indians to improve in many ways. They encouraged them to settle on their land allotments, build houses, and farm and send their children to school. Three of my Aunts and Uncles were teachers in these day schools, which I have always thought were a big factor in helping the Indians to understand the white people and we to understand them. The children learned to speak English and the "three R's;" the girls were taught to sew and cook and the boys to farm and do carpentry work and of course they took a lot of this knowledge home to the parents.

There were Episcopal Missionaries working on the reservation and my Mother did a lot of volunteer church and welfare work, so we grew up in an atmosphere of trying to help the Indians and really loving them and feeling that they loved us. Whenever the Church bell rang we all went to Church whether for a regular service, wedding, baptism, or funeral. The Indians really are religious and this contact with them helped us, while we were trying to help them.

My parents thought that every white person should be a good example to the Indians. I remember we girls wanted to braid our hair into braids, wear shawls and moccasins, chew gum and talk the Native language, but no, we were told we must dress very properly with hoods, coats and shoes and speak English and try to teach the little natives to speak it too.

We were the only white children on the reservation for a long time and as there were no schools except for the Indians we went to the Government school at first. The teacher was Miss Nellie Wright, sister of our Agent, Major J. George Wright, and her assistant was Luther Standing Bear who later became a noted writer, his best books being "My Indian Boyhood," and "My People the Sioux."* Later we had governesses for a while and then went to All Saints

School for seven years. I graduated from the University of Minnesota with a B.A. degree in 1905 but my heart was always with the Indians and I returned to the Reservation as a teacher in St. Mary's Mission School, and as Field matron at Okreek.

I was married in June, 1910 to Edward V. Youngquist of Sioux City, who was starting a bank in the newly organized town of Carter in Tripp County, but continued to do volunteer welfare work among the Okreek people. Public schools were started in Todd County for Indians and white children and I taught for a number of years in these schools.

When my two daughters were ready for High School in 1929 we moved to Rapid City and I continued to work with the Indians. Mrs. Frank Huss and I organized the Winona Club in 1931 which is a Federated Club for educated Indian Women which has become an outstanding Club in the State Federation.

My husband was elected State Treasurer in 1942 and we moved to Pierre and lived there till his death in 1945. Since my husband's death my daughter Ruth and I have lived in Rapid City still doing welfare work among the Indians which we will probably continue to do as long as we live.

*See a listing of his books on page 138.

Rosebud Indian Reservation

Mary Butler Quick Bear
Todd County
1870

The early history of the Rosebud Indian Reservation of South Dakota was closely associated with the lives of a fine old pioneer Sioux Indian couple. They were Mr. and Mrs. Reuben Quick Bear, both now deceased, who spent most of their lives on this far-flung picturesque reservation.

Both were born at old Fort Laramie, Wyoming, Reuben in 1866 and Mrs. Quick Bear, the former Mary Butler, in 1868. They came with their parents to the Rosebud in the late 1870's when the chain of Sioux Indian reservations was first established in South Dakota and the great Sioux nation was moved from Wyoming to these reservations.

They were children together back in the old buffalo hunting days, and both recalled many of these last big hunts with their families in the great encampments of those bygone days. The couple was married at the Rosebud Indian Agency in 1890 by an Episcopal minister, A. B. Clark. To this union eight children were born.

Both Mr. and Mrs. Quick Bear had colorful careers on their native Rosebud Indian reservation and they became widely known as honest, conscientious, hard-working, and highly respected citizens. When Mellette County was opened to settlement Reuben, as he was known by all, was elected in 1911 as one of the first commissioners of the new county. He had attended the Carlisle Indian School of Pennsylvania for several years and was well qualified for his new position.

"Reuben was a good, loyal fellow who was always willing to go out of his way to help both the Indians and whites whenever he could." Frank Perry, pioneer of the White River town area since 1906, recalls. "He was a great friend of our

39

family while my father and mother were stationed as teacher and housekeeper in the Upper and Lower Pine Creek day schools in the Indian Service."

"I can recall years ago when an Indian delegation went to Washington D.C., on tribal business. This bunch, as nearly as I can recall, consisted of Reuben Quick Bear, Clement Whirlwind Soldier, Ralph Eagle Feather, Silas Standing Elk and Hollow Horn Bear. That was the trip on which Hollow Horn Bear got pneumonia and died there in Washington D.C. He was quite a noted Indian and his picture is on some of our nickels today. Reuben wanted me to go along on this trip, but I was just a kid and didn't want to go. Later I wished that I had gone with them.

"When we first settled on the Rosebud in the Indian Service in 1906, there were several Indian trading posts scattered over the big reservation. Some of these were Cut Meat (now Parmalee) Oak Creek (now called Okreek), Wood, Little White River store, and Blackpipe. Reuben finally bought the Blackpipe trading post and operated it for a number of years. Later, after the country settled up, the name of Blackpipe was changed to Norris.

"Reuben was the postmaster at his Norris store for some time. He also served as a clerk at the Rosebud Indian Agency at one time, and once clerked in D. W. Parmalee's store at Parmalee. So in addition to his counter commissioner job he was in the service of the public for many years, and he always came through with flying colors as a loyal courteous, honest, unselfish public servant liked by all.

"Reuben came to the Rosebud as a lad of 14 and grew up with the old timers who are crossing the bar one by one. It seems that there are very few left of the real old timers like Reuben and Grandma, as Mrs. Quick Bear became widely known after she became advanced in years. A good many of my schoolmates with whom I went to school under my father, who taught in Indian day schools on the Rosebud from 1906 to 1922, are also crossing the bar. There are a few left about my age who grew up with me, but when we get up in the years like Grandma, who died at 85, we can expect to be nearing the end of the rope. Grandma saw plenty of hard knocks, I expect, but I never heard her complain and she always seemed cheerful and happy."

After her husband's death in 1918, "Grandma" Quick Bear lived with her children and at her farm home south of Norris until only a few years ago. Then the new ruling whereby Indians could trade their land for other parcels of land or town homes came into effect, and she traded her land for a house and lot in White River. There she continued to live until her health began to fail her, after which she went to live with her daughter at Stamford.

During her residence in White River, Frank Perry was really and truly a friend in need to her. Several times a week he called at her home to visit and to see if she was supplied with wood and coal for fuel. Often she ran out of money between the arrivals of her social security checks and then he would loan her enough to tide her over. And never once did she forget to repay the loan when her next check came.

Grandma lived alone much of the time in her White River home. Occasionally her son, Joe, lived with her, however. She asked her old friend Mr. Perry over for a long visit on the day she was to leave to make her home with the daughter at Stamford. During a previous visit she had told him that she was nearing the end, and the day she left for Stamford was the last time he saw her in life.

The eldest daughter of Gustavus and Emily Butler, she attended the Genoa Indian School at Genoa, Nebraska, and completed her education there during the school term of 1884-1885. She was a long-life member of the Episcopal Church and took an active part in the women's auxiliary and other Episcopal organizations.

A long, unselfish life of devotion and service to her family, friends, church and community was over at last on March 10, 1953, Grandma Quick Bear joined Reuben and they sleep peaceably side by side under their beloved Rosebud's sod in the quiet little Parmalee cemetery amid the everlasting prairies and pine-studded canyons. [By Will H. Spindler, author of *Tragedy Strikes at Wounded Knee*. Vermillion, S.D.: Dakota Press, reprint edition 1985.]

Dorine Smith Bordeaux
Todd County
1887

Once busy fingers sewed intricate patterns of beads in dresses and headbands, and once these busy hands fashioned ceremonial robes of buckskin. Many times too these same hands painted scenes of the mighty Sioux, tall and majestic in their gorgeous feathered bonnets.

Now the ageless enemy of man, arthritis, has stiffened these hands and fingers and no longer is Mr. W. J. Bordeaux able to ply her needle in the delicate patterns of tiny beads that depicted so many events in her early life, or can her fingers be nimble enough to brush in the beautiful colors of the setting sun against which the warrior raised his head and hands in supplication.

All too soon will this wonderful gift be lost, for she has no daughter to whom she can pass down that which she learned at her mother's knee and her children do not possess the talent with which she was born.

A member of the Brule band of the Sioux Tribe, she was born on the Rosebud in June, 1887, Dorine Smith (Wandering Star) daughter of Mr. and Mrs. Todd Smith. From her mother, who was Zenetta Shaw, daughter of Bear Woman and an Englishman, Gerry Shaw, who was a photographer, she is the granddaughter of Chief Spotted Tail, who was one of the first signers of the historic treaty known as the Treaty of 1868. On her father's side she is a descendant of a colonel in the Army. He married an Indian maiden named Kelley, who was related to the Julesburg for whom the town of Julesburg in Colorado is named.

Her early schooling was in the mission school at St. Mary's on the Rosebud Reservation. Later she attended boarding school and finished her education in Rapid City. For two years she worked for a lawyer, Frank Bangs, in Rapid City before going back to the reservation to work for the government at the boarding school.

She married William Bordeaux, grandson of James Bordeaux, French fur trader, when she was 26. The couple lived on a ranch in Todd County until the depression when they moved to Sioux Falls. [From unidentified newspaper clipping]

Myrtle Miller Anderson
Todd County
1895

In 1889 when South Dakota changed from territorial to state government, the change had no effect upon that vast stretch of territory between the Missouri River and Wyoming, and from White River to the Nebraska border. This was Indian Country under the jurisdiction of the United States Government.

For some time the Indians had been restless and angry. About half of their number had not received their ration and supply of clothing. In revenge they overtook the white man's wagon, burned it, stole the horses, and killed the owner.

The Government then sent General Crook to inspect the agencies and to make peace with the Indians. He was to have photographs made of the Indian way of life and to secure those of the very famous chiefs. For this work, he chose John A. Anderson who took a great many pictures of Indian life and of the chiefs. One set was sent to Washington and Mrs. Anderson kept one for himself. They have now become very valuable for they can never be replaced.

His mission finished, he returned to his old home in Pennsylvania. In a few years, he was back on the Rosebud and was bookkeeper for C. P. Jordan. A short time before his return the Battle of Wounded Knee had taken place. After the drunken soldiers had somewhat sobered up, they went out to gather up the dead. Five Ghost shirts were found on as many dead. There are many Ghost shirts in the country and claimed as having been worn in this battle. This is false. These shirts were worn only while the Indians were dancing, but these had not been removed when the soldiers attacked. Of these five shirts, one was given to the agent, Mr. Wright, one to the Colonel, two sent to the Government, and Mr. Anderson got the last.

Two years later Mr. Anderson went back to Pennsylvania to marry his fiancee, Myrtle Miller. After the wedding they left for the Rosebud.

Mr. Anderson, who was of Swedish extraction, was a tall, lean, regular featured, blue eyed man; noted for his integrity, fair and honest dealings, clean in speech, and upright in life. He soon had the absolute confidence of the Indians. Whenever they became disgruntled with the agent, they brought their money to Mr. Anderson to keep for them until called for. Whenever they asked for its return, the money was immediately returned to them.

Mrs. Anderson is of Dutch extraction from near Harrisburg. She has all the virtues and thrift of that hardy people. She is somewhat small of stature, rather plump, and has dark hair and dark eyes.

The raw prairie country was a great change to her from the thickly settled state of Pennsylvania. She entered into the spirit of her new environment, established a pleasant home, listened with interest to the Indian tales, gave them many meals. She perpetuated the tale, mood of life, customs, in a series of poems, under the published title, "Sioux Memory Gems."* The beautiful illustrations are from Mr. Anderson's photographs.

In spite of the difficulties connected with the new country, the Andersons had many happy times. Nearby was the Indian Agency and also the Episcopal Mission. For the most part, the personnel consisted of highly trained, well educated, and intelligent men and women. With these the Andersons enjoyed playing cards and visiting.

Mr. Anderson knew the Government was making great effort to change the Indian way of life and to teach him the white man's ways. He realized that when the old Indians were no more, any of their implements would no longer be made, and many historical objects lost. During the years spent on the Rosebud, he added to his collection. He had no trouble in securing the best objects, for not only did the Indians have great faith in him but he paid them a higher price than other traders on the reservations would pay, with the result the Indians would come from the remote parts of the reservation with choice objects when in need of funds. His pipe collection secured during the years 1889 to 1909 is especially valuable. He once smoked the "peace pipe" with Red Cloud. In 1892 it came into his possession.

He prized his pipe collection very highly for he knew all
the old chiefs and called them grand old men.

Among the many articles are the war shield of Fool Bull,
who was one of Spotted Tail's warriors; the scalp shirt of
Chief High Horse, the extremely sharp knife of Mrs. Crow
Dog which she used in an effort to kill the agent; war clubs
used in the Custer battle; the tomahawk of Turning Bear;
the sinew bow and arrows made by Elk Rove; necklaces
made of bones and plum seeds; elk horn scraper and two
elk horn saddles. These last are very, very rare. There were
scarcely any even sixty years ago and these are now con-
siderably over a hundred years old.

Perhaps the most valuable article is the war shield of
Fool Bull for war shields were usually buried with the owner.
This was obtained in 1894. War shields were made from
the entire hide of the buffalo. It was heated, dried, and shrunk.
The process repeated many times until it was the size of
a man's chest; then covered with cloth and painted with
the likeness of the owner.

There is the war bonnet of Hollow Horn Bear, the last
of the great Brule chiefs. He was tall, handsome and a fluent
speaker. He was chosen to represent his people during the
inauguration of Theodore Roosevelt in 1905. Arrayed in fine
beaded garments, he wore the bonnet in the parade. He made
his last trip to Washington when he rode in the parade of
Woodrow Wilson in 1913. He caught cold while riding. This
developed into pneumonia and he died in the nation's capital.

South Dakota should be grateful that she has this great
collection of over ten thousand fine historical objects in her
possession. It is the finest in America and can never be
duplicated. Gone are the grand old chiefs, the wonderful bead
and quill workers. The old Indian life will never return.

*See page 138 for publications of Mr. and Mrs. Anderson.

Myrtle Miller Anderson

John A. Anderson went from Williamsport Pennsylvania
to Valentine, Nebraska in 1886 with his father who had taken
up a homestead at Sparks, Nebraska which is about fifteen
miles east of Fort Niobrara. He was seventeen years old at
that time. The following year he became an apprentice to a

photographer by the name of Cross. At that time Mr. Cross had a studio at Fort Niobrara, but he soon moved his shop to Fort Meade, South Dakota, where they remained during 1888.

After finishing his apprenticeship Mr. Anderson went back to Fort Niobrara where he started a little studio of his own. While there he was hired by General Crook to accompany him on his inspection of the Indian reservations in South Dakota. Mr. Anderson went along as his official Photographer. I think this may have been in 1889 for the photograph of the Rosebud Agency was made in 1889 and must have been made at that time.

In the Fall of 1889 he returned to Williamsport, Pennsylvania and attended Potts Commercial College. After finishing he took a position in a French studio in Williamsport. He stayed there until 1893. Then he accepted a position with Mr. C. P. Jordan as bookkeeper in his Indian trading store at Rosebud South Dakota.

Just before Mr. Anderson left we became engaged. Two years later he came back and we were married and left at once for South Dakota. That was in the Fall of 1895. There were no fast trains in those days but we finally reached Valentine Nebraska at one o'clock in the morning. I had never been out of the State of Pennsylvania before and when we walked up the dark streets of Valentine, it all seemed pretty strange to me.

We left in the morning with a team and buggy for Rosebud, it was the early part of November but the day was warm and balmy, but it seemed to me like an endless trip as it is forty miles and it took all day. Finally I saw Rosebud in the distance. When Mr. Anderson asked me if I would be willing to come West for no more than two years until we got a start, little did I know that I would be in South Dakota for forty years. But I cannot say, "God kindly veiled my eyes," for my life in South Dakota were the happiest days of my life. I am a D.A.R. and I think my ancestors must have left me a little of their old pioneer spirit.

The Indians were pretty wild then, as it was shortly after the Wounded Knee outbreak. So I had thrills every day. I can remember so vividly when we were driving to Rosebud I noticed a small bunch of cattle running, I said

to Mr. Anderson, "why some big dogs are chasing them."
He looked and said, "dogs, nothing, they are gray wolves."
I had read of gray wolves and how terrible they were, so
expected them to turn on us at once, but John said "they
won't bother us as long as they have cattle to chase." But
I watched from the back of the buggy until we were out
of sight of them.

In 1895 Rosebud had not changed since it was first built.
Our little house was built of boards and lined with ceiling
boards. On Thanksgiving day it had grown very cold and
was snowing. I cooked our turkey in the little wood stove
oven in our little lean-to kitchen, by that time the kitchen
was so cold that we put up a little sewing table in the living
room as close to the coal stove as we could get it, then
brought in cut turkey and put in the middle of the table,
then sat up to the table with blankets around our shoulders
and ate our Thanksgiving dinner, and were truly thankful
for the shelter that we had from the terrible storm outside.
Later we remodeled our house, put in a furnace and was
very comfortable.

Once when I was scrubbing the floor in our little one
window bedroom, it suddenly became very dark. I looked
up and there was a large painted Indian leaning against
the window and trying to look inside. It frightened me but
when I told Mr. Anderson about it he said, "Oh that is
nothing, he was just curious." One evening the following
summer, a thunder storm came up. I went over on the store
porch where an Indian clerk was standing watching the storm,
then I saw an Indian standing on a hill with both arms
uplifted. He was singing a weird song. She asked the clerk
what he was doing. He said, "praying to the Thunder Bird
so the people won't be struck by lightning." That picture
stayed with me for years, so in 1928 when I had my little
book of verses published, which we named "Sioux Memory
Gems," and it was illustrated by Mr. Anderson, I described
that scene to him and he got an almost exact photograph
for my book. This picture was later used on the outside
cover of the *American Forestry* Magazine.

One evening I heard the loud cry of an Indian woman
wailing and going about the hills. I asked someone what
was wrong. They told me that an Indian woman had just

died and she was mourning for her. The next day John came in the house and said, "Remember the mourner on the hill last evening? Well she is very angry, she said that she mourned harder than anyone and all they gave her was a bedquilt." I learned then that it was a custom at that time to pay their mourners.

Later that Summer, John was asked to get several Indians to go with Wild Bill's Show. They all gathered in front of the store and strapped up their baggage before leaving for the train at Valentine, Nebraska. The women all had many dresses on, one slipped over the other, sometimes as many as six. When one dress got soiled all they did was slip it off and lo, a clean dress.

In 1904 Mr. C. P. Jordan retired, and Mr. Anderson and the Hornby Brothers at Valentine, Nebraska bought him out. The Hornby Brothers had a business in Valentine, so Mr. Anderson was made Manager of the Jordan Mercantile Co. so named in honor of Mr. Jordan.

Mr. Anderson always had a hobby of collecting Indian relics. His first purchase was a pair of Indian dolls, bought while he was at Fort Niobrara. He was over 40 years accumulating his collection. When the new Indian Museum was started at Rapid City, Mr. Anderson was asked to loan his Collection to the City, with the understanding that he would become the Director. So we closed out our business and moved to Rapid City. After living there three years, the Indian Department at Washington D.C. bought his collection as they wished to keep it in museums for the Sioux Indians, as they said that it would be a shame to let so valuable a collection get away from them. In the Fall of 1938 we sold the collection and moved to California. Mr. Anderson died in 1948. He never liked California and always longed for the wide open spaces of South Dakota. I am still living in California. South Dakota would never mean anything to me without Mr. Anderson, for he was a part of it.

Catherine Rooks
Bennett County
1880

Joseph Rooks, first being duly sworn, on oath deposes and says; That in December 1866 he married an Indian woman named Tiń gleśka [fawn], a member of the Sioux Tribe at Mr. E. W. Whitcombs cattle ranch on Boxelder Creek about twenty-six miles South of Cheyenne, Wyoming in what is now the state of Colorado. That they were married according to the customs of her tribe and that he gave her adopted mother a horse for her. That he was present at the Indian Council held at Ft. Laramie held in April, 1868 and that he signed the treaty which was made with the Sioux Indians at that time and place. That he lived at the place where he was married until 1867 when he moved about sixteen miles South where he lived for one year. After the Treaty was made at Ft. Laramie he moved with his family to the Whitestone Indian Agency where he lived until 1870 when he moved to Ash Creek East of Ft. Robinson where he lived until his wife died in 1872 about the last of May, she died about ten miles East of Ft. Robinson at the Rosebud Agency. Of this marriage there was born to him three children.

That on the 22 day of February 1873 he married Katharine Robinson a mixed blood Indian woman of the Sioux Tribe a member of the Pine Ridge branch of that tribe. That he was married this time at the Rosebud Indian Agency the ceremony being preformed by the Rosebud Indian Agent, whose name was Robert Cox. After his second marriage he lived with his wife at the mouth of Beaver Creek when he moved back to Ft. Robinson where he lived until 1878 when he moved to the present Pine Ridge Indian Agency where he lived until 1880 when he moved to a place on Little White River on Pine Ridge Indian Reservation about ten miles North of Cody, Nebraska. That in 1892 he was appointed Boss Farmer of the Pass Creek District a position which he held until 1900. All of this time living at his ranch on Little

White River. During the time he was Boss Farmer he lived at Corn Creek Commissary.

In 1903 he moved to his present home one mile West of Redstone Creek and about three miles South of White River. As a fruit of this second marriage there has been born to him fifteen children, [one of them] Rosanna Rooks (now Allen) born in 1880. That during all the time since his first marriage in 1866 he has lived on the Rosebud and Pine Ridge Indian Reservations and that during all this time he has been engaged in the Stock business handling both cattle and horses.

Signed _____

Subscribed and sworn to before me at Kadoka this 24th, day of January A.D. 1910.

_____

Notary Public within and for
Stanley County, South Dakota

Rosanna Rooks
Bennett County
1880

"I was born," says Joe Allen of Martin, "at Fort Laramie, Wyoming, in 1876. My folks used to tell me that I was born in a dugout and raised in the corral. The corral was right close to the dugout so Father could corral the horses at night and guard them from the Indians that were always hanging around the fort.

"Mother was one-quarter Indian and the rest was mostly French. Father came from Indiana when he was younger and before he enlisted in the army most everybody called him the "Major." I don't know why.

"My father freighted from Fort Laramie through Cheyenne to Deadwood. In those days freighters didn't live long, but whether it was because Father was a good friend to the Indians or because Mother was one of them, he never had any trouble.

"I don't remember much about old Fort Laramie," says Allen. "We came east in a covered wagon when I was five. Father worked in Valentine for a while, checking out supplies to the Indians. Valentine was at the end of the railroad at that time and they freighted the supplies from Valentine to the issue stations on the reservations.

"The government was trying to make farmers of the Indians at that time and each family was given horses and cattle, wagons and machinery and harness to start them out farming. Then as soon as each child reached eighteen, he or she was set up in farming the same way. Besides that, every two weeks the Indians were issued rations of coffee, beans, flour, rice, sugar, dried fruits, clothing, etc.

"After we moved to South Dakota, Father worked for the government, building houses along Wounded Knee Creek. Then we moved to Chadron. Father was always writing in his spare time and he and Mr. Hill edited the Chadron *Democrat*.

When the agency was moved from Fort Robinson to Red Cloud Agency (later Pine Ridge), "Major" Allen and his family ran the store and post office until Pass Creek Issue Station was established. The family then moved to the new station and started a store there. The new station later became known as Allen Issue Station in his honor.

At that time young Joe was about sixteen. Helping to run a store was too tame for the boy and he took a job as horse wrangler with the riders taking care of the Indian cattle. He received $30 a month and was paid every three months in gold coins.

"There was a big wild red steer that roamed the breaks from Bear Creek east of Martin to the mouth of Corn Creek on Big While River. We had picked him up several times on roundup but he was big and wild and tough and nobody could keep him from leaving the bunch when he took a notion he wanted to. He got to be six or seven years old and big as a boxcar. In the spring of 1895 Mr. Rooks, the boss farmer at Allen Issue Station, told us that we would have to get that steer this time.

"We got him in with the roundup and he was doing fine until something went wrong. He threw up his head and took off. George Craven and I tried to head him but we could no more turn him than we could fly. It took an awful good horse to stay with him.

"We had our ropes down and finally I got close enough to dab my rope onto him. I only got him by one horn and a front foot, but it slowed him enough so that George could catch up and he got his rope onto a hind foot. We were going down hill by that time, heading for a deep canyon. The horses could barely have stopped themselves the hill was so steep and with that 1600 pound steer on the ropes and trees getting in our way. Then George dodged a tree and gave the steer the slack he needed. He ran right over the top of me and my horse. Both of us had to turn loose with our ropes and by the time I got back on my horse the steer was long gone.

"We found him, though, and oozed him up on top. Then we had a race. The ropes were still on him and snaking along through the grass at about thirty miles an hour. I leaned down from the saddle and grabbed the end of my rope. Then a couple of dallies around the saddlehorn and I slowed him up enough so that George could pick up his rope. We snubbed him to a tree then and Rooks came with some boys the next morning and butchered him.

"Mr. Rooks saved the horns and later gave them to me. I saved them until just the other day our boy, Perry, came down from Rapid City and took them home with him."

In December of 1889, Joe Allen and brown-haired, blue-eyed Rosanna Rooks, were married. Rosanna's mother was a mixed blood and her father, Joseph Rooks, was the first boss farmer in Allen. Rosanna had lived a good share of her short life in Allen, except for five years of school at Wabash, Indiana, two years at Flandreau and two years at Gordon, Nebraska.

Says Rosanna, "They sent me away to school at Wabash when I was only five years old. My older sister went with me. I was scared half to death of the trains and the people and I was so homesick that I spent most of the first two weeks crying. The Quaker teachers were so kind to me and I grew to love them so much that when I left there and came back home I spent nearly as much time crying to go back to Wabash as I had spent crying to come home to my mother five years before.

"I liked it at Flandreau and at Gordon, too, but when I went to Gordon I had so many younger brothers and sisters to take care of (there were eighteen children in our family) that I soon lost track of what the lessons were all about. I couldn't keep up with my classes so I finally told my folks I wasn't going to school any more."

When the reservation was surveyed (about 1910) Joe Allen was allotted a full section of land and his wife, Rosanna, was allotted a half section, all of it south of where Martin is now. As fast as the children arrived each child was allotted a quarter section of land as near to the home ranch as possible. Joe already had a sizable herd of cattle so they did very well until about 1920.

Everything went to pieces then. Prices dropped, a bad winter almost wiped out his cattle and what were left weren't worth anything. Allen sold his land to pay his debts and was unable to buy back again.

"Martin," says Joe, "used to belong to us Allens. Father and my brother, Sam, bought eighty acres of land from John Swallow about 1910 or 1911. They divided it up into lots. Some people moved in. Bill Bayliss and a fellow by the name of Watson started a store here.

"In 1912 Martin and La Creek got into a tussle about which was to have the county seat. Of course, we all thought the proper place for the county seat was here in Martin as it was more centrally located.

"Finally the day arrived to vote on it. Rosanna was about to become a mother again and I waited as long as I could, but the little fellow was stubborn. At last I told them to name him Martin if he was a boy, and I left to go to La Creek to vote. When I got home our boy, Martin, was waiting for me—all dressed up in his best."

Mr. and Mrs. Allen have four children, 20 grandchildren and 31 great grandchildren.

When the Battle of Wounded Knee was mentioned, Allen's eyes gleamed reminiscently. "My father," he said, "was a reporter for the New York *Times* at the time the battle took place. I've heard him tell about it many times. The Indian men were squatting or sitting in front of Big Foot's tent. Father was walking about in the space between the soldiers and the Indians, trying to take down as much of what was said and happening as he could. There was another reporter or two, a priest and the interpreter, a mixed blood Sioux named Philip (Bill) Wells.

"Old Big Foot was sick in his tent with pneumonia. They brought him out and laid him on some blankets where the officer in command could talk to him. The Indians had on their bulletproof "ghost" shirts and they were pretty sullen and defiant.

"The officer was talking to Big Foot through the interpreter when suddenly everything seemed to happen at once.

"The medicine man had just begun to throw handfulls of dirt into the air when a big Indian came charging out of a tent yelling and brandishing a butcher knife. He made a pass at the interpreter and cut off the end of his nose, all but a little piece of flesh and skin at the end. The interpreter grabbed his nose in his hand and put it back on.

"At the same time a soldier was trying to see if an Indian had a gun under his blanket. The Indian shot him through the belly. A soldier slashing open a tent to look for hidden weapons was mowed down. Father and the other reporters and the priest hit the ground and everything busted loose.

"Big Foot was probably the first Indian to die. The soldiers were engaged in a hand to hand fight with the Indians nearest them when the troops turned loose with the Hotchkiss guns, killing almost as many soldiers as Indians. When the Indians saw that their ghost shirts weren't going to do them any good they broke and ran for the hills with the blood-crazed soldiers after them."*

*This interpretation of events at the massacre of Wounded Knee on December 29, 1890 is in marked contrast to that of the commanding General, Nelson A. Miles, commander of the Military Department of the Missouri. Outraged at the atrocities committed by the army, General Miles twice attempted to court-martial the officer in charge, stating, "The action of the Commanding Officer, in my judgment at the time, and I so reported, was most reprehensible. The disposition of his troops was such that in firing upon the warriors they fired directly towards their own lines and also into the camp of the women and children, and I have regarded the whole affair as most unjustifiable and worthy of the severest condemnation."

General Miles testified several times in favor of a compensation bill for the Wounded Knee survivors. "The act, he said, seems to me "of imperative importance and justice . . .to atone in part for the cruel and unjustifiable massacre of Indian men and innocent women and children at Wounded Knee on the Red Cloud Reservation, South Dakota." [Gen. Nelson A. Miles to Cato Sells, Commissioner of Indian Affairs, 12 April 1920. Wounded Knee Compensation Papers, South Dakota Historical Society.]

As of this date (December 1, 1990), Congress has not yet passed such an act, nor has it apologized for the massacre.

FEAR

Side by side with friendship stood fear. But fear stood taller.
[S.R.W.]

Viola Spry Mumby Winget; Bon Homme County, 1883

In October, 1883, Mrs. Isabell Spry and her daughter Viola landed in Marion, Dakota Territory, from New York state on their way to Running Water, Dakota Territory, where the son Vivian had preceded them to prepare a home and get a job.

As we had several hours to wait, I wanted to explore the place but was forbidden to go out alone. The landlady, also from New York state, laughed and asked "Why?" Mrs. Spry responded by saying "INDIANS." She was assured I would see no Indians and was perfectly safe. You see the opinion the New Yorkers had of Dakota.

Helen A. Smith Brown; Brookings County, 1887

When I first came to South Dakota, I was afraid of the Indians. One old Indian woman, called Old Granny, came regularly to see my neighbors and beg for food and clothes. They would invite her into the kitchen and give her a lunch but when I saw her coming to my home, I locked the doors and hid in the closet. I was so afraid of her. My husband had many Indian customers and friends in the store and could talk their language to some extent.

Lucinda Davis; Butte and Harding Counties, 1877

Indians were still a source of danger in the country. In later years Mrs. Davis told of one night when she heard the tramp of horses' feet, coming nearer and nearer. She lay listening with bated breath, hoping if it were Indians they would take their horses and go. Morning revealed the tracks of many horses but those belonging to Davis and Spaulding were still there. Later it was learned that the riders were moving some horses to another range. This incident is one of many that would have struck terror to a fainter hearted woman. But Mrs. Davis remained and did her part in the taming of the wild country.

Jette Hansen; Brule County, 1874

Only three of the [Scandinavian] families stayed in Dakota territory. The rigorous winters plus the Indians proved too much. The biggest Indian settlement at that time was near the mouth of the White River on the west side of the Missouri.

Martha Ellen Mahaffey Bowles; Hand County, 1883

She always hung a lantern high at night so that her husband or neighbors could find their way home. She was desperately afraid of Indians and Indians were frequent visitors, and on one occasion she hid her children in tall slough grass at night.

I Zora Petty Francis; Fall River County, 1890

While living there, one day she and her sister were busy preparing the noon meal, when they heard a commotion outside and looking out the window, they saw a band of Indians with knives and hatchets in their belts, coming toward the house, and of course I Zora thought they had come to kill them. As it was a very cold day in late January, she hurriedly wrapped her three weeks old baby in a blanket, took her two year old daughter by the hand, forgetting to put anything on her or herself and ran the two miles to the marble quarry as fast as she could, to her husband. He thawed the little girl's feet with snow as they were frozen, borrowed coats for them and returned with them to her sister's home. The Indians had been friendly, however, and only asked for bread and beans which her sister had given them and they had gone away happy.

Margaret Lathrop; Charles Mix County, 1882

I arrived on the scene on the 22nd day of October 1882 and held the distinction of being the first white child born in Wheeler and was quite a curiosity to the Indian women who would gather at the house and talk about the white papoose and hold me and play with me until I was utterly spoiled.

When I was a child I just can't remember what terrorized me the most: the fear of Indians coming and scalping us all, rattlesnakes, or the prairie fires that would come sweeping down over the hills to burn off the range, burn up the fence posts and perhaps burn up our winter hay.

Melissa Ann Stewart Oldham; Charles Mix County, 1879
All the other neighbors [except the Joneses] were Indians or mixed breeds . . . Times were hard and Mrs. Oldham spent much time alone, with perhaps a young boy or man to help as Mr. Oldham often had to go elsewhere to seek work. I remember her telling of him spending .a winter in Pierre, while Sam Lindley, then a young man, stayed with her and at one time he had gone to Mr. Oldham's brother's place on foot, to get salt which they had run out of, and an old Indian coming repeatedly to try to get her to trade for something. Then after dark she heard someone coming and on listening, she knew all the boys by the way they walked, she heard it was Sam returning and how glad she was to have him come instead of the old Indian whom she was afraid it might be.

Another time in the old days a man by the name of Moorhead lived on an island and a bunch of Indians got unruly and went there and took his gun and shot a hog and took him prisoner, but when they were going down the river with him a handful of white men scared them and made them turn him loose and give his gun back. Those same Indians stopped at the home of Mrs. Oldham and she locked the door and there was one at each window. She stood in the middle of the room ironing, they were begging for food and finally she thought of an Indian word which meant "not any" which she told them and they finally left.

Anna Wood Berryman; Meade County, 1880
Another time while Mrs. Wallace was out hunting the cow and Mr. Wallace was away from home, two Indian women came to the house and the two girls dragged the baby under the bed, where they stayed until their mother got home. The squaws [sic] were sitting on the door step when she returned. She was so frightened she could hardly get to the house. The Indians often wanted to trade horses and guns for Mrs.

Wallace and the children. Our parents succeeded in making
we children believe it was silly to be afraid of the Indians.
Later I learned they had been very worried about the Indians all the way.

Anna Holsten Berg; Butte County, 1886
Mornings when they awoke, she said, they sometimes
heard the whooping and chanting of Indians engaged in their
sunrise dances. To these people from far-off Sweden, the
Indians were a race of people whom it might be very unpleasant to meet. The stories circulated about Indians were of
ill report – seldom was anything good said of an Indian.
Very likely these four travellers had the feeling that good
luck was following them on this trip because they met no
Indians. But inasmuch as Indians were heard chanting, they
must have been in close proximity. It could be that the
Indians wanted no more to see a white man than a white
man wanted to see an Indian. Had they met, chances are
as favorable that no one would have been molested. The
Indians may have been dancing in religious fervor, alone.
They were not perpetually on the warpath.

Mary Anna Mayer Comes; Hutchinson County, 1884
"I was afraid the Indians would take our baby, so to
satisfy their demands for food I went to the cellar and got
some of Mother's homemade bread and told them to catch
some chickens from the farmyard," recalls Mrs. Comes. "They
still wanted more 'chicks', but were able to catch only two
of the frightened fowl. After the Indians were given food,
they left peaceably," she remembers.

Anna Jorgenson Jones; Turner County, 1884
There were still many Indian trails in eastern South
Dakota in those early days. My father's farm was about
thirty miles north and east of Yankton and seemed to be
in the path of migration from the Yankton Reservation to
Pipestone. We were never too happy when a caravan of Indians would make camp near our well for we had heard many
stories of massacres and scalpings of not too many years
before. It took many years of farming to finally obliterate
the trails as they were deep and many of them.

Nona Smith Saltmarsh; Hand County, 1883
There were many Indians in the country at that time, their trail from Fort Thompson to the Sisseton Reservation was just one half mile from our claim. How primitive they looked, in caravans a mile or more long, with no wagons. Long poles were attached to either side of their ponies, the ends dragging on the ground, and a carrier of hides placed between the poles. They had large numbers of ponies, but many of the Indians were walking, especially the squaws [sic]. There were always innumerable dogs with every group of Indians. I was so frightened whenever these dark-skinned savages came to our claim shanty, begging, that I would hide by my Mother, her apron over my head.

Caroline Stalheim Nelson Weeks; Clay County, 1860
Indians, of whom she was very much frightened, often came to the home requesting food which she sympathetically gave.

Isabel Hubbell Tessin; Day County, 1883
Storms were not the only worries the early settlers had. Fear of the Indians was great. We could not blame them in a way for being on the war path since the early settlers had taken their land from them.

The Sioux tribe traveled back and forth from Ft. Pierre to Ft. Sisseton. They camped along the Elm River on the Northwest corner of our land. There were usually five or six wagons drawn by Indian ponies. The squaws [sic] and papooses would be sitting in the bottom on the wagons with black shawls over their heads. The old Indian braves bedecked with paint and feathers would ride on a board in front of their wagons or ride their ponies beside the caravan to protect their families.

We had heard and read so much about how they would come in the early mornings and kill whole families so when we saw their caravans coming over the hill, we prepared ourselves as much as possible to protect ourselves from them.

On one occasion, after having seen that they were in our midst, Father and my oldest brother took the stand down stairs while Mother and the rest of us children were up stairs each with some weapon for defense.

It was a very dark night and about one A.M. we heard footsteps resembling those of a pony then a fumbling at the doorknob. Father grabbed his gun and went to the door. He had one hand on the doorknob and the other on the gun. He said, "Who's there?" The fumbling stopped for an instant and then began again. Again Father said, "Who is there?" and it stopped again.

Father was a Civil War veteran. In war they gave the warning three times and on the third time they shot so on the third fumbling at the doorknob, Father said, "I have given you warning three times and now I am going to shoot." My brother opened the door while Father aimed his gun at what was supposed to be an Indian. To his great and happy surprise, it was our pet colt.

We found the Indians to be very friendly. They never gave us any trouble, except when they would come to our home to beg for food. We always gave them what we had so they would be our friends.

INDIAN SCARES

The Red Men used to roam the prairies, but were not savage.
Melissa Keene; Clay County, 1870

Evelyn Sturgeon; Sheridan County, Nebraska
In the month of August while we were on a trip to the river with a load of salt, a panic occurred, the story of which we relate in brief as told us by our better half that helped to enjoy it to the full. During the day, word was received that all the settlement on the Blue had been murdered, and from every appearance the Indians would bounce upon the Salt Creek settlement that night. It was nearly dark, wife and children were at the mercy of the neighbors, as they had no team.

Uncle Peter Bellows came nobly to the rescue. With his broad German accent he said, "Mrs. Coax you shall go wid us." Blessed be the name of Uncle Peter forever; but Uncle Peter had his peculiarities. He was a great hand to gather up things, such as old log chains, old plow shares, broken pitchforks, horse shoes (he didn't have a horse in the world), ox yokes, and all sorts of old irons. He was rich in old irons. In packing up to go, Uncle Peter had of course to take the last one of these precious jewels, but in the hurry and excitement he forgot to take any provisions for the family.

When he came for wife he said, "Mrs. Coax we takes you and the childrens but we can take notings else. Vell dot ish so, hurry up mine Got, the Ingins is coming sure." Wife protested that she must take something to eat, and some bedding, and finally persuaded him to take a sack (50 lbs.) of flour and a ham of meat, and a bed, provided she would walk herself. We then had three children, the oldest aged five years, the next aged three years, then Elmer, of whom we have spoken, aged sixteen months. The oldest girl walked, and Nettie was perched upon the load of goods, and wife carried the babe upon her right arm and with the left she carried one end of a trunk a mile and a half or to the ford. The babe she carried the full ten miles, that dark stormy night. Wild with fright they went pell mell.

Imagine, if you can, the terrors of that awful night: the rolling thunder, the lurid lightning, and the mortal dread of a savage foe. Weary and fainting they arrived at Shirley's ranch late at night. In the morning it developed that the sack of flour and ham of meat were all the provisions in camp for a hundred hungry souls, except green corn bought of Shirley, but they had plenty of old irons. It further developed that there had been no hostile Indians within a full hundred miles.

Minnesota, later Dakota:
Louise Green Hammer; Davison County, 1870-1871

It was the time of the New Ulm massacre. The dwellers of Rochester were in dread terror lest any dawn might bring such a visitation upon them; watchers on horseback were stationed to give alarm and the boats of the river were loaded with supplies in order that, should the alarm be sounded, they might take quick recourse to their boats in the hope of safety in retreat. The Indians did not come, but so greatly terrified was Louise that they quickly and frequently thereafter explained to her that the Indians would not attack kind people. One had only to be kind and friendly to Indians and they would be their friends, too. Later, when Louise was growing up on the homestead on the Jim, she had occasion to practice the lesson taught on the Zumbro River.

Here it was that she practiced the lesson of kindness to Indians, learned from the terror of her early childhood.

At the juncture of the rivers, came the hunters and trappers. During early blizzards Indians often stayed for days. She recounted how one day in the spring, after the ice had gone out of the river, came a heavy freeze putting a thin layer of ice across the span. There came an Indian, his squaw [sic] and papoose [sic] and stood across the river from her home. Soon the man got on the horse, the woman took a heavy stick, broke the ice and led the horse across. Later when the Indian had gone on hunting, Louise asked her why her husband had not done the wading through the icy water. The squaw [sic] explained that if he had, he would have to wait to get dry before he could hunt, while she could take her time to get warm around the camp fire, which she built.

Louise spoke the Indian language quite fluently by now, and often sold them needed flour or sugar from the family supply. She had a small scale, and recalled, with humor, that if she, by mistake, put too much of a commodity on to the scale and started to take some out, the Indians murmured and thought she was cheating them. So she learned to dole out a small amount at first, then kept adding until the correct amount was shone on the scale. This pleased the purchaser and she was thought generous!

Wilhemina O'Neill; Faulk County, 1882

The Indian scares were a worry. I remember on Sundays when it seemed relatives and friends congregated at our home, and sometimes wondered if the Indians would go on the warpath, and perhaps scalp everyone, but nothing ever happened.

Selma Buehler; Day County, 1887

Bristol once had an Indian scare. No scalps were taken, though. The only thing lost was sleep. It was shortly after the railroad came to Bristol and a train was "tied-up" there over night. So when the rumor of the roving Redmen hit the town, people crowded on cars and went steaming away. Not everybody though, especially farmers, never heard the alarm and stayed home. Turned out that the Indians were not on the warpath at all; they were just looking around. Wonder if the "refugees" got the rail ride for nothing or if they had to pay a train fare.

Helen Sandve; Day County, 1888

The first year there were rumors that the Indians were coming. John Wickre bought a gun and my father had a gun. The Indians didn't come, they went further east by the lakes and settled down. Fort Sisseton was built in 1864, there were soldiers living there then and waiting for the Indians to show up.

Emma F. Ross Bennett; Edmunds County, 1883

Indian scares were not unusual and one time all the women and children were put on the south train ready to leave any time; later this Indian scare was found to be a false report.

Jessie McGlashan Gunderson; Hyde County, 1883

Indian scares always caused alarm. One time a horseback rider came from Faulkton with the news of a raid. They put the kids and some personal belongings in a wagon. In haste they grabbed the cherished clock, wrapped it in a towel and charged off for the court house in Highmore. When they got there the court house was full so they stayed at Thompson's. Their firearms consisted of one rifle, one shot gun, and some pitchforks. Luckily the Indians didn't come this time, so the family reloaded themselves in the wagon and jogged home. Much to their surprise when they got home what should be on the shelf to brighten their homecoming but the cherished clock. It had been the dish rag that had made the flying trip to Highmore to evade the Indians.

Sarah Ann Cooper; Sully County, 1885

One afternoon a man came to the house and excitedly told us that the Indians were on the war path, and that we had best go to the Rilling ranch where a number of our neighbors were going, and in accordance with plans previously made for such an emergency. It had been arranged to gather a number of families together at strategic spots for mutual protection. Loop holes had been cut in some of the buildings to allow the defenders to shoot the marauders without themselves being seen. The Rilling house was badly crowded, and when nightfall came the people spread quilts and blankets on the floors in the house and in the buildings. Sentries were posted and the hours for the regular relief of them was planned. But no Indians appeared.

Kjerstie Fjeseth; Brookings County, 1873

The economic was such that the husbands had to go away for weeks at times to earn some money, so that the woman was left alone on the wild prairie. It was at one time that a man on horseback came and told that the Indians were on the warpath. It proved to be a false alarm, but caused a lot of fear. One woman said she would jump in the lake before the Indians should get her.

Mary Wallstrum Grout; Miner County, 1875

During the Indian uprising in the mid-eighteen seventies a group of Indians on horseback came along the James River trail which went right past the Wallstrum home. They saw watermelon rinds on the ground that had been thrown out for the chickens to eat, and demanded some to eat. Mary's mother tried to make them understand that she had no more left to give them. Seizing Mary's sister, Hannah, the leader held her on his horse, riding back and forth in front of the home. Mary's mother grabbed the unloaded shot gun threatening to shoot. They went on their way down the trail dropping Hannah a short distance away. She received a shoulder injury.

Kittie Brink Armstrong; Beadle County, 1882

We were on the claim during the Indian scare of 1882. A boy, Milton Wilson, brought the news to us. Bands of settlers gathered for protection at one claim shack. Our bunch sat around and looked scared and fearful of what was going to happen — but nothing happened.

Fanny Macy; Bon Homme County, [1870]

Soon after the folks had left for the party the girls began to hear terrible cries and shrieks. Their only thought was of Indians. They thought they must be scalping someone. Several puppies that were outside cried and tried to get into the house but the girls were frantic and did not dare to open the door. Instead they piled all the furniture they could move against the door and sat in terrified silence during the long night, hearing occasionally a heart rending shriek. After what seemed ages to them the family returned from the party and told the girls that the "Indians" were only coyotes, but they never did forget that horrible night.

Annie Rebecca Farrington-William Rankin
Wedding Picture
Married February 11, 1879

Mrs. Samuel Colgrove; Hamlin County, 1878

Mrs. Poppen recalls hearing her mother tell of many early day incidents. Outstanding among these was the day a band of Indians came through shortly after the white families arrived. The Indians started digging up mounds of dirt, a few feet apart, apparently intended as a trail for other Indians of the tribe to follow. The Colgroves were very much frightened, entertaining visions of Indians on the war path, anxiously waited for succeeding events. But the Indians never came, and gradually anxiety subsided. [They were probably digging wild turnips. V.R.]

N.N.

She has lots of pleasant memories of early days, but she was terribly homesick and frightened when she first came, and remembers one night after she was married, during an Indian scare. Her husband had gone to the school house to drill and she was home alone with her babies, and she heard a horse coming at a terrific pace, and she sat paralyzed with fear, thinking it was an Indian, but it was a man from town delivering a telegram.

Annie Farrington Rankin; Day County, 1882

The Indian scare of one Thanksgiving night: Someone spread the alarm, "Indians on the warpath, coming our way!" We snatched up children and food and ran in our nightclothes to the train whose engine had steam up and ready to pull out when we learned it was a false alarm.

Anna Marie Peterson Gardner; Faulk County, 1883

George (the oldest) was a small baby when there was an Indian scare. Our father was away working on the section. Mother had a young girl staying with her. One night the girl said, "Mrs. Gardner, there is an Indian looking in the window." Mother walked by pretending to be going to the bedroom to see that it was only a horse seeking shelter from the storm. Mother told us this incident many times, always ending up by saying how terribly frightened she was.

Several neighbors had loaded all possessions they could in wagons and drove to a safer place until the scare was

Anna Peterson Gardner
Taken in Montana on 78th birthday

over but Mother stayed there alone with a young girl and baby. She must have known God would take care of them.

Anna and Emma Webb Smith; Beadle County, 1880

They well remember early day scares and fears of Indians. Mrs. Smith recalls how when she returned to Hitchcock following her marriage all the residents of the territory huddled in the one little shack, together with fighting equipment, to ward off a feared Indian attack.

Kate Johnson Boland; Custer County, 1880 (by Lois Miller)

Indian scares were common, but it was more scare than actual hurt. I don't believe my husband was ever really scared of the Indians. When he was away once in a while I had to tend the post office.

Etta Gertrude Sykes; Codington County, 1880

Although we were never molested by Indians, we were alarmed several times by reports that they were headed our way.

Dollie Wilson Dippert; Perkins County, 1893

Mrs. Dippert told of an interesting event in her early life and 1895, when the army called all remote settlers living near the Hills into Sturgis, to be near Fort Meade for protection against the Sioux who were giving the rural people some trouble at that time.

She relates the following story of her trip to Sturgis. "We loaded all of our clothes and most prized possessions into our old covered wagon, and with my father, mother, four sisters, and one brother, we started for the Black Hills. I can only remember crossing Belle Fourche River, and because of my fright, my mother gave me her brown satchel to hold while fording the river."

It took them four days and nights to get to Sturgis. They hid in ravines during the day, and travelled at night as much as possible so as not to be seen by a prowling band of Indians. One evening they heard horses' hoofs coming across the prairie, and thought sure it was a band of the savages, but it turned out to be two cowboys from the "Flying V Ranch," out hunting strays, and stopped in their

La Vicie on her 82nd birthday

camp for some coffee, as they could see the smoke from their supper fire coming from the ravine.

After a few weeks her father returned to the ranch on Rabbit Creek to tend his cattle and horses, but he left the family in the Fort for the winter, returning in the spring for them, as it was declared safe by that time.

La Vicie Marie Kale George; Potter County, 1889

Several times in the early days there were Indian scares, and the men would gather all their weapons together and make ready to protect the settlement. People from the country would come to town and bring what they could with them, sometimes a featherbed on the back of a cow, etc. Once a company of cavalry was stationed there for about three months, expecting an attack.

Christina Anderson Frawley; Yankton and Lawrence Counties, 1870

Enroute from Yankton to the Black Hills on one moonlight night, one of the men accompanying the James Anderson party thought he saw Indians among the horses. He immediately notified Mr. Anderson; at once all the men surrounded the horses. It proved to be a false alarm, as the flies were bothering the horses and in the moonlight the movement of their heads with the manes bobbing up and down, sideways too, looked like Indian war bonnets.

Another tale, Christina's mother brought her favorite rocking chair, which these writers still have in their possession. In the evening around the camp-fire Katrina would have her rocker, and often rocked her small daughter. This group dared not sing in fear of attracting the Indians or highwaymen – so for relaxation and enjoyment, James Anderson would play his violin around the fire after a hazardous day's journey.

She too recalled how the scattered bands of Indians that roamed the Hills surrounding their home would uniquely communicate with each other. How eerie it was to observe how the Indians would signal from the hill-tops: fire signals at night and smoke signals during the day. It was always on such occasions that the men milking their cows had a rifle near by. Her father during the early days hired an Indian scout, thereby someone was able to converse freely with the Indians, and often a few bold warriors would approach the ranch home. On each occasion they were merely hungry and wanted some food. A good meal would be prepared, and these Indians would subsequently be rounded up and escorted to Ft. Meade by the soldiers. There, cared for under military regulations, and later transferred to the reservation.

Kate Van Camp; Hyde County, 1883

The early pioneer days were interesting and occasionally danger was experienced. A large number of Sioux Indians had been located at Ft. Thompson south of Hyde County but they gave no direct trouble. However destructive prairie fires were often blamed on them, claiming they either purposely started them in order to scare the settlers out or that they were careless, leaving camp fires. Fully as many fires were started by careless settlers or by the railroad engines as by the Indians.

Hattie Daugherty Place; Beadle County, 1881

In the fall of 1884 there was a little Indian scare in the community. A neighbor living west of us had been to Miller shopping, while there an Indian was seen in the distance, galloping his horse as though in haste. No one knowing his errand, the observers immediately began to conjecture, and concluded he must be carrying a message for war.

The excited neighbor hurried home and, Paul Revere like, began to alarm the settlers. He came to our house and urged father to get the neighbors to bring their firearms, ammunition and families, and assemble at some house for better protection.

I recall my father's reply — "I don't think the Indians are going to antagonize 'Our Uncle Sam', so we will stay at home and welcome them when they come."

We went to bed as usual, slept undisturbed, with no bad dreams of scalping Indians.

We heard later that a few settlers did congregate at a home, waited all night long, but no Indians showed up.

That was our only Indian scare.

TREATIES

Far from being passive victims of treaty violations, the Native Americans in Dakota successfully defended the treaties they had made with the United States government whenever circumstances allowed. And, except for the Black Hills, the pioneers usually (if grudgingly) accepted the legal limits of settlement. [S.R.W.]

Betsy Himle Swenumson; Yankton County 1870, Sanborn County 1880
In 1870 the family with other relatives loaded a few possessions and went to Yankton vicinity in Dakota Territory, planning to make a home there. But they were driven out by unfriendly Indians. The little company suffered many hardships on their trip back to Iowa. One of the women walked and waded a river carrying her three day old baby.

Mary Jane Gould Weldin; Tripp County, 1880
We saw a great deal of the Little Sioux Indians, who were on the warpath, provoked to anger over the opening of land to settlers near Bonesteel. The settlers had violated the treaty with the Indians, arriving too soon upon the land. The Indians did not allow anyone to cross the river from the east. Some people slept in the cellars because of the scare.

Kristianna Ortness Trygstad; Brookings County, 1869
An expedition representing the Dakota L and Company of St. Paul traveling with ox teams from New Ulm reached Dakota Territory in the summer of 1857. [They] located a townsite near the Big Sioux River in the southern part of the county and named it Medary, in honor of the Governor of Minnesota. It was their plan that this should become the capital of the new territory. Major DeWitt with a group of about fourteen men built quarters and remained through the following winter, but in the spring of 1858 a hostile group of Sioux Indians ordered them away. The whites obeyed

and there was no blood shed. The settlers already had planted some potatoes but the Indian squaws [sic] dug up the seed and prepared a feast. Later after a permanent settlement was established on the same site, settlers discovered relics including household utensils and farm implements that had been thrown into a well and never recovered by the original inhabitants. It was eleven years after Major DeWitt and his men left Medary before the Trygstads came to make a permanent settlement on that site.

The Brookings *County Press* of March 6, 1879, tells of the earliest and biggest scare the Trygstad party had after their arrival in the Medary vicinity in the summer of 1869:

"A short distance from them was seen a large party of Indians passing over a rise of land with ponies and long poles attached, loaded with buggage, squaws [sic], papooses [sic] and savage looking warriors. Their fear was increased by seeing a party of the warriors approaching them. Some of the men caught up their guns and advanced to meet the approaching foe. Slowly and cautiously they approached each other, while the women and children remained huddled together waiting in breathless anxiety the result of the attack. The joy of the party can be better imagined than described, when the approaching savages, instead of rushing them with tom-a-hawks, merely asked for tobacco. The men relaxed their grip upon their guns and gave their visitors a hearty welcome. The Indians were invited to the camp, supplied with the longed-for tobacco and, after a short conversation carried on by signs and motions, the new acquaintances parted the best of friends." [By Marie Trygstad Graves]

BLACK HILLS

The Black Hills Claim is probably the oldest on-going legal battle in U.S. history. It began in 1874, when Lt. Col. George Armstrong Custer led a [illegal] military expedition into the Black Hills and later sent out glowing reports of gold. Miners invaded the Black Hills in violation of the 1868 Fort Laramie Treaty and criminal laws of the United States then in force. In 1876, Congress attempted to coerce a sale of the Black Hills by passing a "sell or starve" bill which required the Sioux to sell the Black Hills or lose their rations guaranteed under the Treaty. When Congress could not obtain three-fourths of the signatures of the males of the tribes as required under Article 12 of the 1868 Treaty, they proceeded to "enact" the "agreement" into law on February 28, 1977.

James J. Wilson, *Valour and Honour in Defense of Country*. Rapid City: Little Warrior Publishing Company, 1983., p. 37.

The next summer [1874] brought more provocation for trouble. Custer had marched into the Black Hills, where, by the treaty of 1868, no white man was ever to go. But the Northern Pacific railroad was in financial difficulties, and locating the gold known to be there would promote investment. Mari Sandoz, "There Were Two Sitting Bulls," p. 61. (MS 565, S1, F1; Sandoz Collection, Nebraska Historical Society)

"We are standing on territory once belonging to the Sioux Indians—that great warlike race, like the Romans, who ruled everything from the middle of Wyoming to Chicago. I wish we had treated them better, in a more noble manner. We are standing on their very land, for which we never paid a cent—just stole it from them and lied about it. Well, these are the things we probably will do something about some day."

A 1940 speech by Gutzon Borglum [sculptor of Mount Rushmore] quoted by Mrs. Gutzon Borglum in Address at meeting of Sioux Memorial Association, Chadron, Nebraska; November 21, 1941. "Sioux Indian Memorials," *Nebraska History* XXII, p.94.

A new treaty was made turning the Black Hills and out to the Cheyenne over to the white man. That treaty was signed by only a small part of the number required by the Treaty of Ft. Laramie in 1868. But it did result in the Indians giving up a lot of high class land the rights of which are still in dispute and in generally accepting life on the reservations . . . Many Indians, the better advised, well knew that the Treaty made in 1876 was not a legal one and theirs [sic] was agitation from both the white man and the Indian to review that treaty and sign a new one.

South Dakota Governor Sigurd Anderson "Address at Wounded Knee, 1956." Wounded Knee collection, South Dakota Historical Society.

A more ripe and rank case of illegal dealing will never, in all probability, be found in our history.

United States Supreme Court, Justice Blackmun, 1980.

Lum McCracken Elshere; Pennington County, 1884

The county school superintendent of Pennington County when I was teaching was the first white woman to enter the Black Hills. She was Mrs. Anna D. Tallant. In 1876 the Dakota Territory was still closed to white people although a few men did slip in to search for gold. That winter Mrs. Tallant with her husband and nine year old boy and a few other men slipped out of Sioux City, Iowa, crossed the Missouri River into Nebraska and from there into the Dakota Territory. They traveled in November and December when the Indians would be in their winter camps and not traveling. Mrs. Tallant wrote in her book that they entered the Hills on Elk Creek and struck Custer's trail through the hills. They followed this trail to a spot near the present town of Custer where they stopped on Christmas day and built a stockade for the winter. The Army discovered they had gone and sent soldiers after them. The soldiers were

within one day's travel of reaching them before turning back.
In the spring a second detachment of soldiers was sent to
bring them out to Ft. Laramie. However, the following year
Mrs. Tallant with her husband and boy joined the gold rush
to Deadwood. While in Cheyenne, she met Bill Hickok on
the street. In a gentlemanly manner he asked her about
the Hills. That was the only time she ever saw him.

After loading on our wagons as many supplies as we
could haul, we crossed the Missouri River by ferry to Ft.
Pierre. After arriving in Ft. Pierre, we began to see Indians.
What interested me very much was the travois the Indians
used when traveling. They took two long poles and fastened
one end of pole to the sides of a pony or a dog and the
other end rested on the ground; they connected the poles
with wood or leather and piled their belongings on this slant-
ing platform and the pony or dog drug the pack. Later the
government issued light weight wagons to the Indians.

We did not see many Indians as they built their huts
and villages along the streams where there was a supply
of wood and water. These streams ran into either Bad River
or the Big Cheyenne. This old Deadwood Trail crossed rather
than followed them.

Jennie Evans Baggaley; Lawrence County, 1877

John Baggaley started for the Black Hills in the spring
of 1875 but was held at the Platte River because of government negotiations with the Indians. He returned to Galesburg
and started again in the spring of 1877.

Mrs. Baggaley and their daughter, Mae, who was five
years old, followed in September of the same year. They
went by wagon train from Pierre. There were still frequent
skirmishes with the Indians. A party had been wiped out
the previous week. Every night one man stood guard. The
last night out from Deadwood as no Indians had been seen
on the trip they decided to do without the night watch.
Jennie Baggaley lay in the wagon with the flap of the wagon
thrown back as the night was warm. The sky was clear,
the moon shone brightly and she thought the sky had never
seemed so near. Suddenly above a rise of ground not far
away she saw the head of an Indian appear. She lay quietly
for a moment and then she saw a second head. She waited

no longer but slipped out of her wagon on the opposite side
and aroused the men. They immediately set up guards and
took every precaution for an attack. The Indians did not
come closer and the next day they drove safely into Deadwood.

Mary Bardwell; Bon Homme County, 1861

Benton spent several years prospecting in Colorado, going to the Black Hills in 1876. He left there because—as
he expressed it—"I want to be able to comb my own hair."
The Indians were making the Hills very dangerous and there
were but very few profitable claims.

Minnie Roach; Clay County, 1876

Her father was a member of the Wagon Train that
delivered supplies to Deadwood during the time the Indians
were on the war path in South Dakota. These men stayed
hidden in the day time and traveled at night in order to
make the trip safely.

Annie Ash Eldredge; Lawrence County, 1876

We went up the Missouri River from Yankton to Fort
Pierre on the "Yellowstone." When we arrived at Fort Pierre,
freight was taken from the steamer, and loaded onto ox-
drawn covered wagons. Other wagons were made ready for
the families going to the Hills. These covered wagons were
drawn by horses, mules and oxen. No less than 100 wagons
were allowed by the government to go at one time, because
of Indian trouble. There were about five hundred persons
in our party.

Charlie Nolin, the mail carrier, traveled with our party
until we reached Rapid City, when he started out alone. Our
party found him killed and scalped by Indians.

Louise Uhlig; Lawrence County, 1876

Early in 1876 Mr. Uhlig brought a party of gold hunters
from Sidney, Nebraska, to the Black Hills, leaving Mrs. Uhlig
at Sidney. During the trip a severe storm at Hill City caused
him to lose a large amount of his equipment.

Mrs. Uhlig, then only nineteen years of age, became very
lonesome for her husband, and wanted to come to the Black
Hills to him, but he did not want her to come until later,

because of the baby, and the fear of Indians. But with courage
and determination she persuaded the foreman of the Pratt
and Ferris freighting outfit, Jim Cury, whom she knew, to
take her and her three month old baby boy, Theodore, with
the ox-drawn freight for Mrs. Uhlig, and a feather bed from
Sidney, Nebraska, to Deadwood.

Mrs. Uhlig rode up on the top of a load of flour, on
a feather bed, just under the bows of the canvas covered,
ox-drawn wagon all the way from Sidney to Deadwood. When
she grew tired of riding in this position she was helped down,
and carrying the baby, sometimes walked for several miles
along the side of the wagon. When she became tired of walking the men helped her on the wagon again, where she rested
on the feather bed.

Each night the wagons circled and a corral was made
as a precaution against Indian attacks.

When the oxdrawn covered wagons reached Deadwood,
July 3, 1876, several of the men riding horseback with the
train left and rode into Deadwood and located Mr. Uhlig,
who came out to meet the train. When he walked up the
street with Mrs. Uhlig carrying the baby the crowd wildly
cheered; they were so glad to see a woman and a baby.

Lillian Clark Ayer; Lawrence County, 1878

When the stagecoach reached Cheyenne, Wyoming Territory, there was news of Indians on the war-path, in fact
they had just brought in a man who had been scalped the
day before. But the journey was resumed and it was not
until the stage coach reached Hat Creek in Wyoming the
Indians appeared. They seemed disappointed when they found
no gold and left without harming anyone.

My mother had very long, heavy hair. It was kept braided
and the braids came below her waist line. This was lucky
in one way but unlucky in another. In the stage coach journey,
lucky because when the Indian scare came the other
passengers braided their jewelry, watches and money in her
braids and thus saved it from being stolen by the Indians.
Unlucky because invariably passengers in a stage coach
became infected with lice and when they attacked her heavy
braids there was nothing to do but return the attack. Her
mother had her sit in the end of the coach each evening,

pull her hair over her head and then pour kerosene through it. She said the lice dropped out by the hundreds.

Annie Cruikshank; Lawrence County, 1882

It was in the early '80's when Grandma arrived by train at Pierre where the railroad ended. From there she got to the Black Hills by way of mule and bronc team. Her destination was Lead, where her husband had a job as master mason from 1882 until 1907. The bronc team that brought her to the west was so wild they had to be roped and thrown forcibly. On the second day out from Pierre the outfit was "attacked" by Indians.

A bottle of alcohol which one man had brought along because he had heard the water was bad, was the cause of the "attack" as the Indians has whiffed the alcohol!

"There were twelve young Indians in the bunch, and they changed their ideas quickly when they saw me," said Grandma with a twinkle in her eyes.

In fact, there were two young ladies in the wagon train that claimed the Indian's attention, but Grandma more than the other because she was almost a platinum blonde.

The other girl, her friend, was a dashing redhead, and the two girls seemed to wield a spell over the young Indians because of their hair. It was strange to them, and they ran their fingers through the silken hair almost as if they could hardly believe what they saw.

The two girls cringed in fear and tried hard not to let on, but the Indians harmed no one in the whole outfit. When the wagon train managed to get underway again, the Indians followed.

To look back and realize a dozen Indians were trailing them, put terror into the hearts of those early pioneers. They kept going until eleven o'clock that night, the Indians trailing along, whiffing the alcohol aroma and wondering about the two unusual looking girls. [By Lois Miller]

Eva Robinson Dawes; Pennington County, 1883

The railroad was built only as far as Pierre; from there they had to go by covered wagon across the Reservation. This was about 160 miles. and took seven long, hot, tiresome days.

The wagon we were in was driven by a hired man, my mother and father riding in a light buggy towed behind. My brother was about a day behind us with the stock and household goods.

One incident occurred to break the monotony of the long days. At Pierre, supplies were bought for the trip, especially big loaves of bread. One night as we were sitting down to supper around the campfire, five Indians rode up, got off their horses, and sat down with us. We were scared to death – the first Indians we had ever seen – and the driver, somewhat of a tenderfoot himself, was as bad as we. If only our brother were with us. We felt we must make them welcome; so Mother took a large loaf of bread, cut several slices on a board and passed it to the one who seemed to be the chief. He, without ceremony, picked up the corner of his blanket, made a huge pocket of it, and calmly swept the whole thing, loaf slices and all, into it, saying simply – "Papoose." Flap jacks served us for bread the rest of the way. [To the Lakota, a host who offers food, offers all, not just a portion. – V.R.]

Addie Robinson Hanley; Pennington County, 1883

How thrilled I was over everything in this new and strange country! The Prairie "Schooners" with their many teams of plodding oxen, the cracking of the long "black snake" whips, the burly drivers and their rich vocabulary of swear words especially when stuck in the gumbo, and the wild riding Indians who scared us to death, took all our bread and thereafter we dined on "flap jacks" three times a day.

When we reached Rapid City we found it to be a truly Pioneer town – small – set deep in the gumbo dominated largely by the cowboys from the great cattle ranges and once or twice a year by the Sioux Indians who came to get their Government rations of flour and to cut tepee poles in the Hills.

One night a party of these Indians about 800 strong got a supply of "fire water" and raised what we commonly call "Cain." The towns people, in terror, sat up all night with weapons ready in case of an attack, however no attack.

Another time when the Indians were visiting us, they put on a war dance, not the commercialized, white – man – sponsored affair of these modern days.

Mrs. Nathan Colman (Amalia Oppenheimer)—1877
Lawrence County

The young bucks* had smeared their bodies with a thin smooth layer of gumbo, wore feather trimmed breech clouts and gorgeous war bonnets and decorated their faces and bodies with weird designs in many colored paints.

My mother watched the dance with interest and then suddenly enquired "Where did the Indians get all those gray tights?" My brother answered "Why those are not tights, just mud smeared on their bodies." Mother didn't say anything but in a few minutes slipped away horrified and shocked. What would poor mother do in this era of nakedness, these days of fig-leaf shorts and microscopic bras?

*Bucks is a derogatory term used in describing Indian men.

Amalia Oppenheimer Colman; Lawrence County, 1877

Mr. Colman, on February 8th, 1877, arrived in Deadwood. By April, Mrs. Colman and small daughter made the long hazardous trip by stage coach to join her husband. The stage coach trip was made by way of Sidney, Nebraska. Bands of marauding Indians frequently attacked the stage coaches in those days, and on the day of Mrs. Colman's arrival in Deadwood, a delay in schedule gave rise to the rumor that the stage had been attacked, so many anxious moments were spent by Mr. Colman and others who awaited its arrival.

Eleanor Waldon O'Keefe; Fall River County, 1881

She remembered, too, the trip they made to the Black Hills by wagon train. They stopped at a post controlled by Indians, and traded with the Indians to remain overnight, but in the morning when they started again, a wagon wheel broke. The Indians did not want them to stay longer, broken wheel or not, and she remembered that they had to give them all the knick-knacks they could find in the wagon to buy the privilege of staying over until they could fix the wheel. One of Mrs. O'Keefe's sisters died on that wagon trip.

Armilda Matherly Gamet; Lawrence County, 1878

Matherly had a road-house or trading post about 10 miles from Deadwood where he did a good business selling provisions to the Indians. The Indians used mostly bows and arrows in those days and some of them were not to be trusted.

One day Matherly took his little daughter with him on a trip to Deadwood for a stock of provisions. He had six little black mules to pull the covered wagon and the trail wagon. On the way back with the loaded wagons they came to a long hill that was slick with ice. Matherly decided to take the wagons up the Hill one at a time.

"Now Mildy you stay here with the trail wagon and I'll be back in a little while and get you," her father told her. The girl waited patiently in the trail wagon. Three wagons loaded with Indian families came along. They could not go up the hill as it was a narrow road with a steep grade on one side and a drop of many feet of the other.

"An old squaw [sic] came up and pointed to me, then to her back and up the hill," Armilda recalls. "I was only five or six but I understood her sign language. I climbed on her back and she wrapped her blanket around us papoose style and took me up the hill to Daddy. I thought it was fun but Daddy was provoked and scolded the Indians for taking me."

"Then the Indians offered to trade a most beautiful beaded blanket for me, but Daddy said, 'Why mercy, no! I wouldn't trade her for all the stuff you have.' Daddy scolded me, too, saying that I must never do that again because the Indians steal little white children." The Indians could easily have disappeared into the rough country with the little girl and she might never have been found. [Rapid City *Daily Journal*, 24 February 1952, by Edith Cole]

ECOLOGY

May Holcomb White; Pennington County, 1879

My dad, two older brothers, and John Sullivan began cutting and preparing logs to build a cabin. Ed Crossett, with his team of horses and mowing machine, started mowing hay. It was through cutting down trees to make the cabin and mowing the hay that we learned that the Indians did not approve of us or of such proceedings, as it would ruin their hunting grounds and deprive their ponies of the best grazing places. However, the men kept on with the work until the cabin was completed, one room sixteen by sixteen, with hewn small logs, or large poles for roof, with what is now known as rammed earth plastered heavy on top the poles, which surprisingly shed rain very well, also a very heavy strong door also being made of hewn poles.

While these men were still working on the cabin a band of Indians came to where Ed Crossett was mowing hay and scared him so badly that he unhitched one horse from the machine, jumped on his back with harness on, and fled, leaving the other horse still hitched to the machine. My dad saw him ride away and expected him to return after dark, but he never did and we never knew what became of him. The horse he left at the machine we used as a saddle horse until he died of old age, a very kind, faithful animal and the first horse I ever rode.

As soon as the cabin was finished, the other men began putting up hay. One day while they were all out at work a large band of Indians came to the cabin. My mother saw them coming and she closed and bolted the door. They were dressed up in fine buckskin beaded robes with painted hawk or eagle feathers in their hair, also streaks and figures painted on their faces. They looked in through the two small, high, open windows, and talked to, or at my mother. She could not understand their language at that time, but could understand that they were very angry about the men cutting down

87

and hauling away the hay. She knew something about paci-
fying Indians. She had a fire in the cook stove and had
just baked bread, so she made two large kettles of coffee,
poured it out in cups, bowls and cans, and set it, with a
lot of sliced bread, on the high window sills. When they
had eaten and drank it all they thanked her and went away,
never bothering any of our family again.

Laura Belle Walker Gamet; Fall River County, 1889

It was a long time before we had visits from anyone
except our Indian neighbors. Living on the trail leading from
Pine Ridge Reservation to what is now our county seat,
Hot Springs, we were constantly seeing groups of these first
settlers on their way to the place where they had bathed
in the springs for untold years. Many times I was alone
with my small children, Joe and the other men being at
fields far from home, when I would look out and notice tents
pitched in front of the house.

I would never hear them come, especially when our window and door were closed, they came so quietly and put
up their tents so quickly and as quietly. Later in the day,
some of these wayfarers would open the door and walk in,
their moccasins giving no warning of their visit. Perhaps
I was kneading bread or washing diapers. I would turn and
there would be several red-skinned visitors. I would offer
them chairs. They would sit beside the fire and just sit there,
saying nothing. No word at all, unless it was to request
something by Indian words, signs, and gestures.

Once three or four men stopped on their way to Hot
Springs. As was often the case, only I and the babies were
at the house when they walked in. After sitting silently for
fifteen or twenty minutes, the older man asked for
"Wakalyapi." He pointed to a shelf where I kept groceries
and a few pots and pans. But I did not know what wacoloapy
was. I picked up several objects, holding them out to him.
He shook his head each time. Finally he pointed to the coffee
pot.

I thought he must want coffee, so I put a pound of
coffee in a paper sack. Wrapping it carefully, tying it with
a bit of strong twine, I handed it to him. My visitor shook
his head even more vehemently than before. He showed me

by gestures, imitating the way water is poured into a coffee pot, and blowing on the coals to make fire burn, that he wanted me to make some coffee. So I made a pot of coffee and poured out a cup for each of the guests.

"Caṇhaṇpi," grunted the older one this time. He looked around, saw the sugar dish and pointed to it. I gave them sugar for their coffee, serving them from the blue-and-white sugar dish which had been one of our wedding presents.

"Asaṇpi," the old Indian demanded now, smiling broadly and pointing to a covered pail of milk near the stove. I was glad it was not yet sour, as I hastily poured some into a small glass pitcher and took it to them.

But that was not all. The next request was for "aguyapi," which I did not know at that time meant bread. It was easy to understand, though, when he showed the form of a bread loaf and motioned as if slicing it. This time I opened the oven and broke off great pieces of bread which I had baked for a previous meal.

After they had finished their bread and coffee, one of the men walked to the shelf and poured the remaining coffee into his pouch, so as to take it with him. He reached into his wallet, took out a handful of silver, and paid me. Then they walked out, got on their horses, and rode away to Hot Springs.

"And weren't you frightened?" one of my little nieces once asked. Indeed no. I have been accustomed to Indians all my life, and have never had reason to fear them. They were always our friends. Even as a child in Iowa, the Winnebagos would come to work in the timber. I was taught always to be kind to them, as they often came to the house to trade. I have tried always, too, to remember they were on this land long before any of us came. They never made much trouble until soldiers tried forcing them away from their beloved hills, their abundance of wild game, and sheltering woods.

I recall the year of the Indian outbreaks, [1890, the massacre at Wounded Knee] when the government issued guns and ammunition to our settlers, ordering all women and children taken to Buffalo Gap, where soldiers were stationed. Two of the neighbors had new babies, but they put beds in the wagons, placed mothers and babies in the beds, and drove to Buffalo Gap — twelve rutty miles, and the Cheyenne river to ford.

Little damage resulted from this outbreak. At the end of the trouble, it was found the Indians had killed some of our cattle for food. We have been friends with the Indians since then.

What I admired about the Indians was their custom in regard to killing game. They never killed for sport, as some white men do. They dried their meat and kept it for winter use, using the skins for robes, tents, and shoes. Sometimes I think of those soft robes when I see the deer today, jumping our fences, and seeming to come and go at will in our ranch pastures.

Marguerite Driskill; Harding County, 1878

Jesse Lincoln Driskill, son of Marguerite Driskill, (famous Driskill ranch workers) reported that when in Fort Sill, Oklahoma, he saw fifty-eight acres of buffalo hides stacked as high as they could be thrown from a wagon, waiting for the hide buyers. [Marguerite Driskill, *Rapid City Daily Journal*, 9 August 1959, p.18]

Sarah Ann Klebsch; Spink County, 1879

One time at about the age of fifteen years as I was walking through the woods along the James River, my attention was attracted to some wild grapes overhanging the water on the opposite side of the river. There were several large rocks in the river and I determined to cross the water on these rocks in an effort to get the grapes. The water was deep and the current very swift and in watching the water I became dizzy and fell into the river. I sunk to the bottom and remember just how it looked down there. In a short time I came to the surface and someone soon grabbed my collar and I was pushed forward by this person who was swimming behind me.

When we reached the shore I was pulled out, stood on my feet and shaken severely. This person then disappeared in the thicket. He was a very tall, erect, young Indian man who had rescued me. I was not aware of his presence at the time I fell into the water and I never knew the purpose of the shaking. I always felt, however, that the Indians were my friends and found them a very interesting people.

Another time while walking through the woods I chanced upon an Indian skull lying on the ground. In the branches of a nearby tree were the other bleached bones of the Indian skeleton. It was the custom of this people to wrap their dead in blankets and place them in trees. Flood waters the following spring washed the skeleton from this tree and all traces were gone.

One morning, not long after we came to Dakota, I looked out across the prairie and saw what I thought to be a huge herd of sheep. I watched it for several days and decided to investigate. I started on foot in that direction. The distance proved to be much farther than I had anticipated when I started, as one could see many miles across the prairie. I came closer and I found that my "herd of sheep" consisted of bleached skulls and bones of buffalo. At least 100 of these animals had been slaughtered by white hunters for their hides only; the meat having been a total waste.

Actions such as this could not be tolerated by the Indians. They were justified in defending themselves from people who showed so little consideration for them and their property which they have cherished for so long.

Indians were a very conservative people. They never killed for sport. If they were in need of meat they would kill only enough to satisfy their needs. They considered the buffalo, antelope and other game theirs, much the same as the farmer of to-day considers his herds and flocks. Their rivers and streams were well stocked with fish and yet the Indian and his family were always amply supplied with what they needed.

SCAREDY-CATS

Fear, so strongly planted in the white women who came to Dakota territory, made them behave in rather strange ways at times. The accounts of Iva VanLoon King and Aetna Williamson Tarbell are humorous when read from the Indian's perspective. It's sad that their communication with their Dakota neighbors was never close enough for them to understand the subtle Indian humor that could have eased them out of their fear. [S.R.W.]

Iva VanLoon King; Marshall County, 1877

In 1881, Captain King with the Steamer, Milwaukee, was stationed permanently at Chamberlain, a promising young town less than a year old. His third son, then a lad of about twelve years, loved to swim, fish and hunt. He soon learned the language of the Sioux and made many friends among them. He spent considerable time west of the river in Indian territory and knew every hill, creek and valley there. He often thought he would like to make his home there if the land was ever out. So in February of 1890, when the land west of the Missouri was opened officially for filing, he on his little black Indian pony, made a mad dash across the river on the ice to stake the first claim in Lyman County. However the land of his choice was north of the Correction Line and the Government survey went only south of that line so he had to squat to hold his claim until it was surveyed. This quarter section of land was later to become my home for fifty years. Here my six children were to be born and raised.

But this is away ahead of my story so we will return to Eden where my father has just arrived and after a few days' rest we started for our home in the country.

Every quarter section had a family on it so neighbors were close but many Indians roamed the country and the nights were long and lonesome with only the call of the coyote or the owl to break that dark silence.

So it happened one cold winter day in December of 1885 while I was busy washing baby clothes in the kitchen, leaving my baby girl of about six weeks asleep in the adjoining room, that my mother's intuition prompted me to look to see how my baby was. Imagine my feelings when on entering the room I found four big Indian Braves warming themselves and one bent over my baby in her cradle. I tried to pick her up but before I could reach her he had taken her up and wrapped her in his shawl. All Indians, both men and women, wore shawls to keep them warm. I flew to the door and put my back against it, shaking my head and saying, "No." Four big Indians staring at me and one with my baby wrapped in his shawl. They seemed to consult with one another but I could understand only the one word, "Papoose."

I knew it was an Indian custom to enter a home all unannounced and beg for food or anything that struck their fancy. So I thought fast. How could I reclaim my baby girl? Spying an unopened plug of chewing tobacco my husband had placed on a corner bracket within my reach I seized it and began trying by sign language to barter it for my baby. After some very serious consultation on their part the Brave took the tobacco and gave my unharmed baby girl to me, with a big "Ugh." Then they left the house and I was much relieved to see them go down across the meadow and disappear in the trees along the river.

That evening when my husband came home he told me how Flying Eagle and three of his friends had crossed on the ferry (the river didn't freeze until in January that winter) and Flying Eagle told him how they had stopped to admire his pretty papoose and how he had held her in his arms. Years afterward he still talked about it and laughed at my holding the door against four big braves. It all seemed very funny to him but I can assure there was nothing amusing in the incident to me at the time.

My impression of the Indians was also very permanent. The Indians were everywhere, but I had no fear of them, only pity and compassion. The Braves with their long black hair in braids interwoven with gay ribbons or strips of bright material, the Squaws [sic] with the papooses strapped to their backs with a shawl. The little boys and girls, men and women all with buckskin moccasins and always their silent, expressionless countenances. How I wondered what was in their hearts.

I remember one night when my parents awakened me and carried me out of doors saying, "Listen, you may never hear this again." In the distance, maybe many miles away could be heard the rhythmic beating of the tom-tom. My parents told me it was an Indian war-dance, that the Indians did this when they were unhappy and they wanted me to remember it.

Aetna Williamson Tarbell; Codington County, 1878

All day they followed the railroad as nearly as possible. Their progress was hard and slow as the frost was coming out of the ground. That evening, as they were sitting by the camp fire, they saw in the distance what they thought were Indians; however it proved to be two young men in a light spring buggy on their way to locate land near "beautiful Lake Kampeska." The government grant with the railroad read: "to the Sioux river" while beautiful Lake Kampeska was 4 miles farther on!

The next day the young groom and his bride travelled for some time, and then came in sight of a sod shanty. It was the first they had ever seen. As they neared the shanty two men came out, one tossing his hat into the air, and shouting something which the Tarbells thought was a warning to keep away. But the nearer they approached they discovered this man was calling: "A WOMAN! A WOMAN!"—and they greeted them most cordially.

Mrs. Tarbell was soon to find that this cottage in which they were living, was built on the very edge of the Indian Reservation, and the Indians were allowed to come to the Lake for fishing and bathing during the months of May and June. These Indians as they passed the cottage loved to frighten this young bride by reaching thru, as yet, the paneless windows, or, pounding on the floor, and doing many other things to frighten her. So Mr. Wiley, owner of the cottage, fixed a long pole, so whenever Mrs. Tarbell would see the Indians coming, she was to hang a white cloth on the pole, then Mr. Wiley would come over to the house. He had lived among the Indians many years and could speak their language. Quoting Mrs. Tarbell: "However, many times I would be working and turn around and there would be two or three Indians SITTING in the cottage – they were SO noiseless and sly!

"One time I hung out the signal, but, they came in before Mr. Wiley could come. They were holding their hands high above their heads and making strange moans and groans while coming nearer and nearer to me until I was backed into a corner. They kept saying "Minni, Minni." Mr. Wiley came and spoke sharply to them. They tried to make their peace by saying: "Poor white squaw sick of "minni" meaning "water" – come down on white squaw's head." The occasion for their concern was the large hole that had been left in the roof for a chimney which as yet had not been built.

"Another time two young squaws came with a parcel about six inches square wrapped in newspaper and handed it to me. As Mr. Wiley had told me never to accept anything from them, I shook my head and motioned for them to take it back to their tepee. After much insistence, they left. Two hours later Mr. Wiley came to our cottage and said: "What have you done to the Indians?" I told him what had happened. Then he said: "You will have to go over to their camp and make your peace with them for they are angry." So I went shaking hands with each one while Mr. Wiley talked to them. I do not know what he said to them, but they never offered me another gift." [It was an insult to reject a gift from a Dakota. V.R.]

The young squaws wore calico dresses, the young bucks, men's clothing, and the old squires and the chiefs wore blankets.

Mrs. Tarbell loved to ride horseback, so one day she bargained with an old Indian for his pony – finally getting it for $15.00. The old Indian tied the pony to a post and left. When Mrs. Tarbell attempted to go near the pony, he reared, broke the rope and away he flew over the prairie. Much to Mrs. Tarbell's surprise, about two hours later the old Indian came back bringing the pony. He made Mrs. Tarbell understand that he would hold the pony while she petted him and fed him sugar. This completely won over the pony

who would always come when she would call him. So each
morning after the work was done, Mrs. Tarbell put up a
noonday lunch and rode over to where her husband was at
work. [By Mrs. L. J. Shaw]

FOOD

CHIEF RED CLOUD, 1890: For some time our rations have been falling off gradually. I have never been told that that was the wish of the government. None of the treaties made by the government with us since 1868 have been fairly fulfilled, but our rations have been cut down more and more every year and former delinquencies were not made good. The past two seasons have been so dry that we could raise little or nothing, and the rations were so scant we were obliged to kill our own cattle to keep us all from starving to death. A great many had no cattle and those that had were obliged to help them, therefore we cannot increase our stock cattle. In consequence of these hard times many of my people got weak and sick from the want of a proper quantity of food, two hundred and seventeen (217) of them dying since the fall of last year from starvation.

[Quoted in T. A. Bland, "A Brief History of the Late Military Invasion of the Home of the Sioux." Washington, D.C.: The National Indian Defense Association, 1891, p.20]

In 1889 Congress reduced appropriations for the subsistence and civilization of the Sioux to the lowest point reached since the agreement of 1877, viz. to $900,000, $100,000 less than the amount estimated and appropriated for the two preceding years . . . Such diminution certainly should not be allowed, as the Government is bound in good faith to carry into effect the former treaties . . .

[Sixtieth Annual Report of the Commissioner of Indian Affairs to the Secretary of the Interior, 1891. Washington: Government Printing Office, 1891, pp. 134 and 137.]

This action of the Department, following immediately after the successful issue of our negotiations, can not fail to have an injurious effect. It will be impossible to convince the Indians that the reduction is not due to the fact that the Government having obtained their land has less concern in looking after their material interests than before. It will be looked upon as a breach of faith, and especially as a violation of the express statements of the Commissioners.

Report of the Sioux Commission, 24 December 1889, quoted in 1891 Report of the Commissioner of Indian Affairs, p. 134.

Sophronia Payne; Beadle County, 1881

Indians often came to their homestead and held out their arms to be filled with food.

Ida Mae Potter Zickrick; Miner County, 1881

One time when Mrs. Zickrick was home with two small children and had just finished baking bread, some Indians came along in their wagons. They used to travel in groups and always had loose horses following their wagons. This time the Indians were quite disturbed because they had to move from the north side of White River onto the reservation on the south side of White River. They walked right into the house without knocking; this was their way. They talked their Indian language which Mrs. Zickrick did not understand. She talked to them and they did not understand her. They wanted her just-baked bread but neither could understand the other. Just then a cowboy came in off the range, and when he learned what the Indians were after, he sent them on their way.

Sigri Watnaas Gronseth; Marshall County, 1883

This was Indian Reservation then. Sometimes an Indian group could be seen coming across the Prairie, and they would stop to ask for food. The settlers would try and have a little to give them, and then the Indians would go on their way. Most of them were friendly Indians. Soldiers were stationed at Fort Sisseton, so this helped to protect the early settlers.

Clara Ann Ashman Jones; Hughes County, 1895

Hazel remembers that when she was a small child Indians would come to the door for food when her mother and she were alone. The mother always gave them some and they went peaceably on their way. There was quite a little Indian traffic between Cherry Creek and the Rosebud Reservations. The Indians in their striped wagons with their extra ponies and dogs following traveled up and down the trail along Brave Bull Creek which was about a city block from the house.

May Bowman Billinghurst; Spink County, 1879

There was an abundance of game: prairie chickens, wild geese, ducks, antelopes and occasionally buffalo meat, brought by the Indians who came to get fish from our trap which the men had placed in a riffle in the river below the house. Drifting Goose and his band had been assigned to a reservation north of us at a place called Armadale. They were frequent visitors and friendly but they objected to being given the suckers from the fish trap and insisted on pike and pickerel.

Augusta Elizabeth Weinert Engelland; Davison County, 1882

Lots of Indians still roamed this territory passing through here. They often would camp nearby. They would beg for food and various other things. One incident was that an old Indian chief called "Old Oueaha" came to her home many times and begged for home-made bread. If the bread was fresh in the oven or not baked yet, he would hang around until it was done. He was given a loaf or two of fresh bread, and then would go on his way again.

Sarah Congdon Fargo; Clay County, 1864

The old stage road went past the homestead and many Indians stopped and enjoyed grandmother's "Johnny Cake" and sorghum molasses. Many times the braves, rolled in their blankets, took over the downstairs of the cabin and slept as "thick as flies" on the floor. They teased my father by asking to trade "papooses."

Emma F. Ross Bennett; Edmunds County, 1883

Indians and gypsies often had camps near the town. She never refused to give food to people coming to her door and living not far from the railroad many tramps came for hand-outs.

Mrs. Jessie Andrews Sherard—1876
Turner County

Minnie Herrington; Shannon County, 1888

For sixteen years they lived on the Pine Ridge Indian Reservation, twenty miles from Interior, where they leased some land from the Indians.

"As we lived in the Badlands there were times when we didn't raise anything to speak of. The Indians would never steal from me and I always gave them food when they were in need." When the government loaned the Indians money to buy cattle the Herringtons had to move off the leased land.

Amelia Houser Hoard; Lincoln County, n.d.

Their daughter Amelia always remembered that in the fall of the year, during hog butchering time, the Indians would come down from the north to eat what the white farmers discarded. They made their camp on a creek bottom.

Jesse Andrews Sherard; Turner County, 1876

Jessie remembers clearly one incident with the Indians. The neighbors were threshing at her father's place and most of the men had returned to their work after eating dinner when two big Indians walked right into the house, leaned their guns on the table, sat down at the table and started to eat. Eating greedily and grunting at each other they were quite a sight. After finishing they motioned and made signs indicating they wanted food to take home with them. After Mrs. Andrews gave them some they took their guns and departed. During all this time Jessie said that she and the other children stood back in the corner and watched with wonderment and fear.

Mary Ann Mansfield; Pennington County, 1883

An interesting and rather humorous event took place on their wedding trip in October [1884]. The way to Pierre was through the Great Sioux Indian Reservation, over the same road which Mr. Mansfield entered the Hills by stage the year before. They camped out three nights enroute, the men sleeping under the wagon and the women in the wagon.

Mrs. Mansfield had baked a jelly cake for the trip, and it was to be the treat of a meal at Peno Springs. She had placed the cake on a blanket preparatory to serving the meal

when the wagon was surrounded by a group of curious Indians who were encamped nearby. Thinking to be polite and
nice to the visitors, Mrs. Mansfield cut the cake into thin
slices and passed it to the nearest Indian, expecting that
he would take only one small piece. Instead of that, he raised
a corner of his blanket and with a quick movement swept
the whole cake off the plate, wrapped it neatly in the blanket
and departed. As soon as the surprise and chagrin over the
incident had passed, the humor of the event prevailed and
much joking took place. [Again, to the Lakota, a host offering of food meant all of the offering. And one must understand that in the reverse circumstance, they would do the
same. Generosity was a strongly practiced value. −V.R.]

Hila Freeman Wallace; Fall River County, 1887

Just a few days after Bedford was born, an Indian squaw
[sic] came to the house begging. Mr. Wallace let her come into
the house where he and the two older girls were about to
have the noon meal. He asked the squaw to eat with them
and when he passed the bread plate to her, she took it and
emptied all the bread into her lap. Each time she could get
hold of the plate she did the same thing. Mr. Wallace finally
stopped putting bread on the plate. Instead he would get
up and cut a slice when the children wanted more.

After the meal the squaw [sic] heard the baby cry and
wanted to see it. She took him up and held him, and exclaimed
about him in her Indian way. Of course, no one ever knew
what she said. This episode was very frightening to Mrs.
Wallace as she was afraid the Indian woman would hurt
the baby and maybe take him and run away. However,
nothing serious happened from this incident.

Jennie Bean Sanders-Piner; Douglas County, 1882

For sport we played many outdoor games, hunted for
agates, especially after prairie fires and not infrequently I
joined the Indian women, who with the braves now and then
came into the neighborhood, in search of Indian turnips which
they taught me to dig, peel with my teeth and also I learned
how to prepare the roots for moccasin laces. I still have
a turnip in my collection of flora, and also many agates.

STORIES OF SITTING BULL AND TRADE

When they had nothing, the Dakota asked for food. When they had something, they traded. [S.R.W.]

Alice Ashcroft Moseley; Harding County, 1884
One of the oldest friends of the Ashcrofts was the famous Sioux Indian leader, Sitting Bull. He often visited them and bought butter and chickens from Grandmother. One day he came to buy potatoes from their garden. Grandfather was busy and did not want to take the time to dig them, so his daughter Ethel, ten years old, slipped away and dug a half-sack of potatoes and dragged them up to the house for Sitting Bull. He was so pleased that he promised her a pony, and soon a little bay horse was delivered to her. He was named "Two-John" and she had him until she was married to Jack Jacobs in 1896.

Mother's name was Alice Ashcroft. She taught school at Minnesela* near Belle Fourche. Later she taught at Capitol, Montana, just over the State line. She was here when the families were alerted to the Indian uprising of December 1890. A fortress was constructed on top of a bluff on the west side of the Little Missouri. It was called Fort Sourdough and held sixty people. It was occupied shortly before Christmas. Men would go from the fort each day to tend to their stock. One man stood guard during the day, and two guarded at two-hour intervals during the night. The teacher and Greenup Moseley was there with his gun to protect the group as they walked. The older boys called the group "the Pilgrims going to church." The alert was called off on Christmas eve, and school was discontinued for the rest of the winter. In January, 1891, Mr. Moseley and Miss Ashcroft were married.

Families nearer to Camp Crook had gathered at that settlement for safety from the Indians. Several men went

to the Ashcroft home to see that they came in; but Grandfather himself refused to go. He said, "I have never harmed
the Indians and they will not hurt me." The rest of the family went in to town; but when it was over no one had been
harmed.

The town of Camp Crook, though somewhat shrunken
in late years, is still there on the Little Missouri. It got
its name because General Crook had camped there one winter
during the earlier Indian campaigns. When I was a child
we used to go out to a bank near the river and explore
the caved-in dugout of the General, examining the things
which had been left and finding small articles scattered about.

*Mni sayela means red water.

Maude D. Ogden; Lawrence County, 1877

Another time stamped on my memory was being taken
to a corral where several Indians were camping with their
horses in the lower part of Deadwood, and were here as witnesses in a murder trial. The bucks [sic] gathered around my
good friend, Col. Dona, a newspaper man, and he called their
attention to my long braid of hair. Lifting it up, he asked
the interpreter how Sitting Bull would like that. I was a
bit nervous but they all laughed and shook hands and said,
"How."

Eleanor Schubert; Hughes County, 1881

In 1886 Sitting Bull came down the River in a flat boat
on his way to Washington to see the Great White Father.
He landed at the foot of Pierre Street and sold his signature,
which was an X, for a quarter. I was having a class of
piano pupils at the time and they all rushed down to the
River to get his signature in their autograph albums.

Mary Damberger; Campbell County, 1883

[She] emigrated with her parents to farm seven miles
south of Herried . . . When a schoolgirl she and four other
white children were hired by the government to attend school
west of the river with Indian children of Sitting Bull's band.
They were to help teach the Indian children the ways of

the white man. Mrs. Damberger also cooked for the Indians.
[Aberdeen *American News,* n.d.]

* * * * *

Jane Macy; Bon Homme County, 1880
... the Indians used to stop to try and trade off cloth
for chickens or meat.

Mary Vondra Bouzek; Hyde County, 1884
None of the family could speak English. Rose Kozel,
a neighbor girl, was working in Highmore and if Grandma
Vondra wanted something she would get Rose to interpret
for her. There was a Bohemian settlement in that locality
so they got along without the English language.

In the early days Indians would come across the prairie
with two or three wagons and their families. It would be
nothing unusual to see an Indian walking along side with
a bar looking for turnips which they ate.

They were very good, the turnips. In those days it was
all open country, very few fences. They would pitch their
tent near the place especially if they bought a critter with
a lump jaw from a farmer. They would get it cheap. They
would take care of the meat before moving on. They also
traded their beautiful moccasin for some farm product. They
were always friendly but I was scared of them. I was burned
brown from the sun by not wearing a sun bonnet and mother
would say that they would mistake me for one of their kin.
So I would hide under a feather bed until they would leave.
[A cow or steer with lump jaw (a growth on the face) was
a cheaper price because it could not be sold at market. The
meat was fine, there was nothing wrong with it. −V.R.]

Jennie Flowers; Bon Homme County, 1881
The Indians were not hostile in those days but at first
the family was very much frightened when dozens of them
would come at a time, asking for food. If food was not given
to them in a few days they would come with articles to
trade. Mrs. Eglestone often had samples of yarn ribbon or
calico for them to braid in their hair or candy or cookies

for the children. She was over six feet tall, and the Indians liked her. They planned to buy her when they could get enough ponies. She accepted many gifts from them, though she always gave them something in return. The more bright and sparkling the more pleased they were. However, when any of them had an overdose of fire-water, they would retreat before her revolver which she never hesitated to display with stern warnings. It often seemed wise for her to hide from them when they came near and pressed their faces against the windows. Usually if they did not see her they would go away. She was never afraid of anything, and so loved to ride horseback far and wide over the hills and prairies around Chamberlain.

Alice Bauerly Astleford; Jones County, 1909

Sometimes Indians would camp across the road by the dam. More than once neighbor boys sold Alice's pet dog Rover to the Indians. He always managed to chew the rope and come home.

Minnie Berge Brakke; Moody County, 1876

We used to have visits from Indian squaws [sic] and one time we kept one over night. They usually peddled wild plums or grapes in the fall of the year and in exchange they got bread and butter and whatever else was on the table. They would ask for a paper for this purpose.

Bessie Bagby Lumley; Sully County, 1884

There was always thought of Indians and sight of them was quite frequent. Bessie often saw them passing the house on their monthly trips to the Cheyenne Agency for rations, sometimes as many as seventy-five wagons in a row with squaws, papooses, and dogs in the back. They often stopped to get warm and to trade trinkets for food . . . At the age of nineteen Bessie visited her grandparents in Kentucky and they were amazed to find that she did not talk or act like a savage having lived so long in the Indian country . . . Among other memories of a life time Mrs. Lumley remembers that she knew only one Indian who was mean and he was Old Black Hawk. She remembers hearing of the death of Sitting Bull and she has a picture in her mind of Calamity Jane

waddling out of a saloon in Pierre dressed in a dirty Mother
Hubbard dress.

Laura Kentopf Warner;

As a little girl I was always afraid of the Indians that
traveled through the countryside wanting to trade blankets
for watermelons or dead cows.

It was not uncommon to meet and trade with Indians
from the several tribes of South Dakota, and Mr. Harris
recalls that an old Indian friend of his was exceedingly proud
one day when he was able to purchase the gayly-bedecked,
plate glass enclosed and ornately carved, discarded hearse
of the then local undertaker, into which he proudly loaded
his wife and several children, and set off across the western
prairies. [Ella T. Wilson scrapbook, unidentified news clip.]

Katherine Holleman Palsma; Bon Homme County, 1878

They lived in a log cabin on this pioneer farm. This
farm was located on the route of the old stage trail going
from Sioux City to Rapid City, via Fort Randall on the
Missouri River. Mrs. Palsma states that she can still recall
vividly seeing military wagons drawn by three mule teams,
guarded by soldiers, bringing the money for pay day at Fort
Randall. The soldiers were stationed at Fort Randall following the Civil War to help prevent uprisings among the Indians on the Dakota prairies.

The Indians often visited the pioneers on Coffee Creek.
The people would feed the Indians and the visitors especially
loved to eat drippings of grease by the spoonfuls. The whites
would trade food for yard goods which the Indians had gotten from the government. This material was a pretty plaid
goods called lindsey. Mrs. Wynia would make dresses out
of this material and would also make trousers and other
clothing for the men out of other yard goods.

Minnie Berge Brakke; Moody County, 1876

We used to have visits from Indian squaws [sic] and one
time we kept one over night. They usually peddled wild plums
or grapes in the fall of the year and in exchange they got
bread and butter and whatever else was on the table. They
would ask for a paper for this purpose.

Hannah Johnson Oakes; Moody County, 1879

It is not surprising that these early pioneers had their scares. Mrs. Oakes tells about the time she got quite a scare in her home when she came out of her bedroom into the living room and there sat a big Indian on a chair by the door. She summoned her courage and spoke to him; he had decided to just stop in for a while as he was passing by. She felt better after he went on his way. The Indians around their home were of the Sioux Tribe. They were not hard to get along with after you understood them. Mrs. Oakes had an exciting experience with an Indian woman who wanted some grain. They told her she could have one-half a bushel, she didn't like that and came back to the house and said she would "Nepoe" Mrs. Oakes. In the whiteman's language "Nepoe" means to kill.

The Oakes got along very well with the Indians who had a trading post on the river bank at the edge of Flandreau. They traded with them right along, chiefly produce for clothing, in fact they kept little daughter Minnie in clothes for two years. Some of the clothing the Indians had was what they called hickory shirts for men.

Mrs. Walt Ashley; Charles Mix County, 1885

This dwelling was close to the trail the Indians used going from Lower Brule to the Yankton Agency where they received their government issue. As they all went at the same time, there seemed no end to their wagon train. Mother used to trade chickens and eggs with them on their return from the Agency when they had something to trade. Mother gave many an Indian a meal. Sometimes stragglers came along. As they wore moccasins, you never knew anyone was around until the door opened, an Indian came in, closed it, backed against it and said, "How." They were always friendly, and we children were always interested in them. The squaws [sic] and Indian children seldom came to the house. They never said a word.

Bertha Beuther Buhler; Yankton County, 1878

Our land was very close to what is now Charles Mix county, known then as the "Yankton Sioux Reservation," and which was a vast tract of prairie that stretched out as far as the eye could see.

The Indians were always friendly with us and used to camp in our yard for days at a time. They would try to trade us government shoes and good woolen blankets for a chicken or two. These articles were all stamped with "U.S.I.D.," United States Indian Department, but the folks used to say it meant "You Steal, I Divide." There was a law against them selling these goods. They used to eat the potatoes they received from the government for planting, so their agent had the potatoes cut up in pieces like you plant. They told mother "Potatoes, good. Cook nice now."

It was during the years we were gone that the Yankton Sioux Reservation was opened for settlement. The Indians had the first choice, and I'm sure they were both very happy to get home.

Amelia Martha Stimson Lowe, an early Pioneer Daughter of South Dakota; picture taken when the family resided in Parker, S.D. trying to get a start in life.

WORK

Mary Bardwell; Bon Homme County, 1861

The hotel was on the wagon road from Yankton to Fort Randall along which the freight traffic was heavy, and the ranchhouse (as it was called) was the stopover from Yankton. The two girls had to work very hard and were assisted at times by two Santee Sioux Indian women called Betsy and Jennie who came across the river in a canoe.

Amelia Martha Stimson Lowe; Clay County, 1873

Father "dickered" with a Frenchman who had a copper colored lassie for his lady, and paid $300 for a set of dilapidated log buildings, located at a Government Stage Coach Ranch at Bijou Hills. Here, father and mother "squatted," and here, among friendly Indians and frontiersmen, with mother the only white women for 50 miles, and unarmed, they entertained the gangsters and freighters alike, with closed ears and silent tongues.

One night Father was away, and Mother was alone with the little boys, when there was a knock at the door. She "heard" it was Indians, and let them in out of the rain. A buck [sic] and two squaws [sic]. They squatted by the fire until morning, then left. Many of the squaw men [sic] were jealous of men with white wives, and mother always answered a knock at the door so they could at least put up a fight before they got a rope around Father's neck.

Emma Evenson Enger; Buffalo, Hand and Hyde Counties, 1887

Frank had come with his family from Norway . . . then to Fort Thompson where his father was a blacksmith in the employment of the Government. After living at the Fort for nine years they moved to a ranch in Buffalo County. Frank had gone to school at the Fort and spoke the Indian language well.

There was a hotel there which I took over and ran, doing
practically all the work myself. Many of our boarders and
roomers were Indians and they became our good friends.
Frank had the job of caring for the horses. It was one of
his duties to have a team of government horses ready at
any minute for the use of the doctor or nurse who made
many trips over the reservation to care for the sick Indians.

Roxanne Heffelfinger Mehner; Brown County, 1883
We rented a house in Malta; a son Earl, was born
November 16, 1898. We lived there until the following spring
and during those months we hired a poor old squaw to do
our washing for us. We called her "Queen Bee." She had
her blanket strapped around her waist and she never took
it off while she stood and rubbed the clothes on the board
but would let the blanket drop down from her shoulders.
The blanket was of government issue and if she lost it, she
probably would not have received another one until they were
issued again. She and another squaw [sic] come nearly every
day and they were so stealthy that they would be inside
the house and standing beside the closed door before we
realized they were there. "Queen Bee" asked to see the baby
and wanted me to give him to her and she was hard to
convince that I did not want to give my baby to her.
The following February 5th, 1900, our second child, a
son Bernard was born in the log cabin and I was fortunate
in having Dr. Clay attend me at his birth. When he was
six months old, I became sick and we hired an Indian girl
to help with the children and she was with us only one day
when she come down with scarlet fever and then we all had
it. There was a scarlet fever epidemic and several deaths
resulted from it.

May Green Holmes Krueger; Campbell County, 1886
St. Benedicts Mission, which was just across the river
from our store, did so much for the Indians in the way of
education, religion, etc. The Sisters of this mission taught
many subjects such as cooking, music, painting, dramatics,
etc. The church and school were both very wonderful. The
boys were taught carpentry, farming, and taking care of
livestock. There were three priests, two brothers, and several

Sisters or Nuns. One of the priests wrote a hymn in the Sioux language and I have heard the Indians sing this song. Many have beautiful voices with much volume and harmony.

Our customers were made up mainly of Indians with a scattering few white people. Our store was on the East side of the Missouri river about one mile south of the South and North Dakota state line. The Indians lived on the Standing Rock reservation of the West side to the river. We had two row boats to go across to get them in so they could trade at our store. They were mostly Sioux Indians and since it was almost impossible to hire anyone that could speak the Sioux language I had to be in the store most of the time.

JULY 4 CELEBRATIONS

By 1890, South Dakota had a well-established tradition of Indians and settlers sharing July 4 celebrations. Red Cloud was in Oelrichs, Drifting Goose and his band were in Aberdeen, and Sitting Bull marched in the Bismarck Independence Day parade that summer before Sitting Bull was assassinated and 300 Indians, mostly women and children, were massacred at Wounded Knee. [The big question for me is, how did these peaceful ties of friendship between Indians and whites get severed in four months, and who did it? — S.R.W.]

Agnes Euphemia Ramaga Auld; Aurora County, 1882
One fourth of July, Oacoma had a celebration and two tribes of Indians were camped on the bottom land south of the town; my father took us down to see them.

Emily Meade Riley; Douglas County, 1881
The first Fourth of July celebration ever held in Douglas County was indeed a colorful affair. Many ex-service men of the Civil War period had come to the wilderness to mend their broken fortunes, among them a fifer named Hosselton. He had several sons who could really play the bugle and drums. About 10 a.m. on the morning of the Fourth, we heard them coming over the hills in their lumber wagon playing the national airs in a way that made the echoes resound. We thrilled, wide-eyed to the first strains of martial music (or any other) that we had ever heard. We hurried to get started for the wonders of a celebration.

The Yankton Sioux Indians had been invited for a feast. They had been gathering for several days and the prairie was dotted with white tents. I thought the whole tribe was there. The celebration opened by the singing of national airs. Then followed the Hosselton band, the reading of the Declaration of Independence and an oration by a young lawyer, John T. Matthews, who had come out from New York. He chose for his subject "Ridpath's Hamilton." I've heard many orations since, but none so outstanding as this early day contribution.

114

The Indian parade followed: Braves in their war paint and bonnets on horseback, nude save for their breech clouts and feather headdresses with their bodies painted in hideous designs, which was a little frightening to those who had never seen anything like it before. They rode fast and yelled and whooped as if getting ready for war.

Several steers were butchered and the feast was on. Most of the celebrants brought their lunches, as eating places were limited. Pink lemonade was $.05 a glass. No ice was available and the lemonade was about the same temperature as the hot July day. After the feast, the Indians put on their war dance with their tom-tom music. The Indian women put on what they called a "squaw [sic] dance" a sort of shuffling affair making a circle into which they dragged by-standing young men to dance with them, much to the merriment of all.

A bowery floor had been constructed, some fiddlers located and an afternoon dance was under way. Never before had I seen people dance and I thought it the most graceful performance I had ever seen. The ladies wore Gretchen dresses with huge sash bows at the back. Bustles and skirts were in vogue then and the bustles elevated the skirts slightly at the back making a dip in front. They were made of lawn, ankle length and very full skirted and picturesque. I sat and watched them for a while wondering how they could possibly find their way through the mazes of a quadrille or how to know what the prompter's directions meant. Little did I think that a few years later I'd be going through a similar performance.

Two nines of ball players were marshalled from among the celebrants. There was no grand stand, no benches, no shade. It was no fun to sit on the grass in the hot sun with no better protection than a parasol or umbrella so naturally there was a limited number of fans.

Another attraction was the horse races. There was no special track, no entrance fee and any nag could enter the races. There was betting to be sure, but it was light. Nobody was too flush with money and nobody knew the other fellow's horse.

We went home before sunset, somewhat reluctantly. We had hoped to stay for the promised fire works but this was deemed unwise and we mustn't think of it. Such was our

first public entertainment. We now had something to talk
of for weeks to come.

May Green Holmes Krueger; Campbell County, 1886
When July 4th rolled around, La Grace had a big celebration with Indian dances. They built a large bowery for the
entertainment and where people could dance. This bowery
was covered with branches of trees which grew so plentifully
along the little creek that was close to the town and along
the Missouri River which was only about a mile distance.
They danced to their own weird music and tom-toms, singing their many war songs.

Lulu Lee Mooney Traut; Fall River, Hanson and Mc Cook Counties, 1884
While in the Black Hills there occurred the last Indian
outbreak. In the summer before it commenced, I, with my
family, attended a Fourth of July celebration at Oelrichs
where some hundreds of Indians were camped (I was always
told more Indians than whites) in their tepees. The men were
in war paint. I still recall the men on their ponies with the
splotches of bright red, yellow and blue on their bodies and
the squaws [sic] with heavy shawls on their heads and kegs
strapped around their waist to carry the water they used
from, I suppose, a nearby creek. Chief Red Cloud made the
main speech of the day through an interpreter.

Later General Miles was called out with troops and the
Battle of Wounded Knee occurred not very far away. At
one time all the near-by settlers were housed a few days
in a building at Smithwick as it was feared the Indians might
break through and we were in their probable path. The
Government issued guns and shells to them. The guns were
returned but I still have a few of the shells in my possession.
We were very near the railroad so saw troop supply trains
go by.

VISITORS

To not walk right in was to demonstrate distrust; to not take all that was offered was an insult; to not feed the hungry was unthinkable—such was Dakota etiquette. [S.R.W.]

Ella Jenney; Hutchinson County, 1884

I will tell you about my first Indian caller. One morning Mr. Jenney had gone for a load of hay from the school section, the same place the school section is now. There was a lot of "fire hay" grown there then. They told us the hay in some parts of the section was so high a man on horseback could get lost in it. When we said we burned hay, it wasn't just the fluffy hay we usually feed stock, but that tall stuff that took a little power to bend and twist. Mr . Jenney said not to take it off the top of the stack or water would run in and spoil the hay, but to just pull it out. I thought some of the stems went from one side of the stack to the other. Well, he had gone away for hay and I thought I was all alone. I had set bread, not with the quick rising Red Star or Fleischmanns. What a problem we had trying to keep bread warm overnight. I was busy when. . . . . Why! There was the door coming open. I felt almost paralyzed. Then a dark face peeked around the door. "How!" "How!" and a big Indian came in.

I was polite enough to set a chair for him, but he didn't take any notice of it, but went around the room looking at things and looking back to see if I was watching him, and I was. He was a middle aged man. Over his coat he wore a braided leather whip, a blacksnake whip, for a belt, with a big butcher knife stuck inside it. He looked at things and smiled and hummed a little tune. Then he was interested in Mr. Jenney's double-barreled muzzle loading shotgun, with the shot and powder pouches hanging on the wall. He motioned for me to give him some, especially the little brass caps that went with them. I shook my head no. He was

not insistent, but asked for something one kneaded with
their hands. I showed him I had the bread that wasn't baked.
I had part of a loaf; I wrapped it up and gave it to him.
Then he noticed the sugar. I found a sack and emptied the
sugar in it, but he wanted the sugar bowl too. It was part
of that set I had just bought of that handsome clerk in
Dixon's store in Scotland. I shook my head, no. Well, he
finally went away and I surely tried for a long time to not
let any one slip up to the house without my seeing them.

Stana Everson; Brown County, 1879

On the trip to the homestead where Mr. Everson and
his two brothers "squatted" a year earlier, a band of Indians
detained him for a considerable time to listen to the music
of his violin.

Marie Fermstad Ekern; Moody County, 1878

The Sioux Indians lived on the plains and in nearby
settlements around Sioux Falls, Flandreau, and Pipestone.
They were mostly migrating bands who traveled to their
sacred rock quarries at Pipestone. This pipestone rock, while
buried in the ground, was soft and easily shaped into peace
pipes, various tools, jewelry, and trinkets much prized by
the Indians. After a time exposed to the air, this rock would
harden into a red granite-like rock. The Pipestone quarries
were guarded by the Indians, and the white man was excluded.

The Ekern homestead was located near the customarily
traveled route between Sioux Falls and Pipestone. These
migrating tribes could be seen for miles, coming and going.
Dad and Mother usually had ample warning of their
movements. Most of the Indians were friendly and did not
bother the settlers. Sometimes they stopped for water, then
continued on their journey. Mother said only once did they
give her a bad time. That day Dad was away from home,
and seeing no man around, the squaws [sic] entered her home
and stole all her precious sugar, flour, and coffee. If there
were men around, the squaws [sic] would not stop. (Another
good reason for having a man around the house.)

The Pipestone Creek, located about a mile from the
homestead, was a source of supply. It furnished a limited
supply of wood, but game animals were in abundance; deer,

elk, antelope, snowshoe and cottontail rabbits, also buffalo and game birds in season. These were used for food, and the skins provided warm clothing. Wild plums, chokecherries, grapes, and some edible roots could be found growing along the shore line. It was also a source of water during periods of drought when the shallow well Dad had dug by hand would dry up. It furnished an occasional fish, a swimming hole during the hot summers, and a place for kids to explore to their hearts' content. In the winter it was a place to skate and ride the sleds. Ice was cut and placed in the ice house at home for use during the summer. I don't believe we realized at the time how important the Pipestone Creek was to our lives.

During the haying and harvest season, Dad usually had a hired man to help with the work. Sometimes they were young Indian men whom Dad would recruit from the Indian School in Flandreau, or maybe transit laborers who followed the harvest across the nation.

Catherine Maud Boland Arbuckle; Pennington County, 1879

The Indians traveled from reservations in South Dakota to those in Montana and one route was by the ranch. They generally camped on the river near by. They were a source of worry to her. She didn't know how to talk or deal with them and most of the early days she was afraid of them. Although there were no uprisings then, only peaceful migrations, it hadn't been too long since there had been battles and massacres. They stopped at the house when I was only a day or two old and an old squaw insisted on rocking me. Mother was afraid that she might steal me and breathed easier when the lady caring for us made the Indians leave. They were always begging for food and she would give them anything they asked for to get rid of them. Dad often teased her and said they probably called her the Woman They Could Work.

In later years a group camped near by and let it be known they had a sick baby, so mother went to the camp to see what she could do. She found the baby had a severe cold, so made a syrup from some onions the Indians had. This medicine seemed to help the child and when they left they gave mother the onions so she would have them in case her own children got sick. Thus the fear of Indians was gone, and she always visited with them whenever they came by.

Clara M. Bolster Thorne; Minnehaha County, 1872

There were some interesting experiences with the Indians as they used to pass through from Flandreau. One experience which puzzled Mother was on a cold day. An Indian came in and sat down by the fire, not speaking, and after awhile left. Then another one came and sat awhile and left. Then another, and another. I do not know how many came but at last their leader, the only one who could speak any English, came and explained that they wanted to get warm but did not want to frighten her by coming all at once, so decided to come one at a time.

Agnes Euphemia Ramage Auld; Aurora County, 1882

One night we were getting ready to retire when we heard someone walking outside on the lawn. My father went to the door and discovered old High Otter, an Indian who was quite a beggar. It was found that he wanted an old felt hat for a foundation for a war bonnet or headdress. My father found a hat and High Otter went on his way and we went peacefully to bed.

She was the only woman for miles around who had a sewing machine, so her first visitors were women who came to make their baby clothes at our place. These sewing affairs helped in other ways than getting the children clad; they had fun too.

She also brought her organ from her home in Iowa and was a novelty in this country. The Indian Reservation was about five miles away so the Indians seemed to be always travelling by our place. Either to go hunting or fishing. They had a kindly feeling towards the folks as Father was their friend. The Indian women liked to hear Mother play the organ, it was an instrument of mystery to them. She also sewed for them and many a calico dress was made by mother for an Indian woman. They were so grateful to her for this, that [they] would bring her gifts of bead work, or venison they had killed near our place.

There were eight children in our family. I was the oldest and was born February 9th, 1889. Fourteen months later, the second child was born. At this time the Indians we knew so well were in a war-like mood being previous to the Battle of Wounded Knee. So many Indians were holding meetings near our place. Finally the neighbors asked for some protection and through the efforts of Father and his immediate neighbors, soldiers were sent to our locality from Fort Meade, South Dakota. The neighbors came to our place to be near the protection of the soldiers. Naturally all this confusion and the uncertainty of the behavior of the Indians was hard on Mother, so as soon as she was able to travel, she left for her home in Iowa with my sister and I. She remained there until this Indian trouble was over.

Margaret Heil Becker; Dewey County, 1917

I can remember the first summer we were on the farm we had a really good crop. Wheat was cut with a binder at that time. I was sent out along to shock grain on a forty-acre field. You can imagine how fast the binder got away from me. I'd set up a shock, sit down and cry, and go again. I remember an old Indian man named Charlie Face came by and pitched in and could he shock grain. At that time my folks didn't know Indian folks very well and they said he had to come in to eat. After he'd eaten his fill, he went home and again I was left alone. The next day both Mom and Dad came out and the grain was soon shocked.

The first year when they had the Indian Fair, the Indians would come past our place, a caravan maybe two miles long, wagons, horses and what have you. We kids didn't get to go to town to the fair as it was too far.

Mrs. L. W. Riffle taken on her 62nd birthday

FRIENDSHIP AND ASSIMILATION

Beyond friendship, many of these early settlers learned from the Indians and adopted their ways. [S.R.W.]

Mrs. Iver Mathiesen; Hamlin County, 1881

Father came home one day and said, "Mother, what do you say if we go and get a farm of our own?" "Yes," said Mother, "that is easy to say, but how can we buy a farm? We have no money." "Don't you know that north of Watertown they are opening up for homesteading on the Sisseton-Wahpeton Indian Reservation?" said Father. "We can get a homestead of 160 acres by living on it five years or holding it seven years and then paying $2.50 per acre to the government." "I hate to leave all our good neighbors and relatives and go into new country, but I'll leave it to you, Dad," Mother replied. "I left good old Norway and friends before and now I'll go where you go."

When neighbors heard of my folks' plans they tried to talk them out of leaving. I remember one man saying, "Why do you want to go up in that Indian country?" "There are some good Indian people, too, no doubt," Father replied. "We'll get along. I want so very much to have land of my own."

The next day we went up to the post office and store at the Sisseton Agency, one and a half miles away. Here I had a chance to see Indians. As time went on I became acquainted with several Indian boys.

Ethel Fish Parrish Riffle; Charles Mix County, 1884

Other incidents I remember so well, were the wagon trains of Indians, hundreds of wagons going to White Swan to the fall festival. They camped just outside Castalia and George Kirk (our editor at that time) would come to the school house and take all the children to visit their camp. About daylight we could hear them having their song service. There was usually a minister with the train.

123

Julia Mattison Amsden; Grant County, 1880

Julia and Cassus told interesting tales of the Indians. An Indian man worked for them. He had a wife and a son. They pitched their tent across the road from the farm house. Mother envied the squaw when it came time to clean up the house. Instead of scrubbing floors and doing the many other difficult tasks in connection with keeping a house clean, the squaw would pick up her tent and move it to a patch of fresh clean grass and her cleaning was finished.

Olive Luella Seipp Sauder; Hamlin County, 1888

Ralph, Olive's brother (born Jan. 27, 1881) went to school at a mission but as it was too far away Olive didn't go to school. There were Indians in the area and during the summer in moving from one camp to another they would stop near the ranch. Olive used to play with two little Indian boys. She remembered one as named "Charlie." They would cook with prairie dog grease (which smelled awful) over an open fire. They would make something that looked like noodle dough and the other would hold her arms out in front of her and "roll" the dough back and forth on them. The cooking smelled so bad Olive remembered always standing on the side of the fire that the wind would blow the smell away. ["The prairie dog . . . is eaten only under stress of famine." Joseph M. Cook's notes on "Electing a Chief," 29 December 1885, South Dakota Historical Society]

Eva Martin; Codington County, 1879

Mr. McIntyre was often visited by Indians while working in the fields. He never had any trouble with the Indians but he always kept a supply of small gifts and trinkets to give them on such occasions.

Jane Rooker Breeden; Stanley County, 1892

On another occasion a young girl came to ask Mrs. Breeden to visit her mother. The family had lost a newborn baby and the mother, who was of Dakota blood, was disconsolate. She had taken coyote poison (strychnine). While the immediate danger was past, talk of self-destruction persisted. Family and friends said all they could, including the fact that the other children were to be considered. At length

Mrs. Breeden remarked that their father (a white man) probably would feel that his children must have a mother and
might marry again, perhaps a white woman. The lamenting
ceased, then the mourner sat up, called for brush, comb,
and looking glass, and began to arrange her hair. There grew
a feeling of respect and admiration between the two women
that was to last a lifetime. [By her daughter, Marjorie Breeden]

Myrtle Mary Moore Williams; Day County, 1882

The railroad came only as far as Webster so everything
had to be taken to Fort Sisseton by mule train or ox team.
Drivers were usually Indians.

The Moore home was built only 10 rods from the trail.
Soldiers were always going back and forth between the fort
and Webster. Her brothers worked as civilians at the fort.
They had charge of the clerical work.

It was a very impressive sight the day the white soldiers
were marched out and the Negro troops moved in.

Indians were camped around the country hunting and
fishing in the numerous sloughs in that part of the country.
The family was very much amused by an Indian coming
to the house one time and borrowing a shot gun shell and
a kettle. He was surely optimistic. The Indian tied a white
cloth around his head when he went duck hunting. They
could never figure the reason for this.

There was a famed Indian Scout at the fort. His name
was O'Ketchum. Jim King was his white man's name. He
was a pure blood Indian and often came to visit the brothers.
He was skilled in tracking soldiers who had deserted and
in hunting game.

Minnie Slack and Sophia Slack Johnson Bucklin McCaughey; Brown County, 1878

Minnie was the tallest of the girls, with blue eyes and
a fair complexion. She, to, was a beautiful girl and had many
suitors. The Indians called her "Haska," The Tall One.

Bob Love ran the Waubay trading post and was "sweet
on Sis" (older sister Margaret). He arranged a party to go
to Enemy Swim to watch the Indians dance. They all rode
in a wagon with boards across the box to sit on. The Indians
didn't want an audience and were sulky, wouldn't dance. They

were well acquainted with Bob Love, of course, and found
a good way to get even with him. They must have had beans
for dinner. Anyway, they seemed to have lots of windy ammunition. Two or three at a time, they would saunter up
to the wagon, "pop gas" loudly, wander away while other
gassy fellows moved up. Bob Love was so embarrassed and
so mad at those Indian boys for spoiling his outing. [By
Margaret Slack Fuhrman]

Lillian White Drew; Hyde County, 1884

Indians from the reservation came past our house when
they came into town. They came with their complete family
and a horse. Long poles hung from the horse's bellyband
(the big end next to the horse) and as the poles dragged
through the sand they had skins fastened from one pole
to the other to make a shelf to carry their luggage. At certain times of the year they would bring in wild plums and
I had been told that if I was a bad girl my Mother would
sell my brother Walter for a bag of plums and so when
I saw the Indians begin to file past I would put Walter
under the bed and then sit on the edge of the bed to protect
him. He was three years younger than myself.

I still have an interest in Indians. Chief Joseph was
a good friend of my Fathers and he would come to talk
in the Bank and he was quite impressed with my long red
hair and freckles and would hold me and caress my hair
while they talked, my Father told me. I remember the lovely
beadwork done by the Sioux Indians. We had quite a nice
small collection of the work. I remember a lovely hand made
beaded squaw doll—several sizes of turtles—moccasins etc.

N.N.

We made friends with some of the older Indian people.
They were trusty and honest. They told us about the plants
found on the prairie they used for medicines. Also the fruits
and berries found in the draws and along the rivers, which
made delicious jams and jellies.

Alice May Nancarrow Knight; Lincoln County, 1874

On their arrival [in Canton in the spring of 1880] they
found only two other white families: The Kimballs and the

Hilmars. Many friendly Indians came to visit them, however. Among them Sam Finley, Adam Stafford and Horace and Adam Greeley.

The John Arytman family, newly arrived, had no shanty to move into. When their Indian neighbors heard of their predicament they came down with ponies and sleds and took the Artmans to the home of Edwin Phelps, where they spent the winter. Mr. Phelps was the first Indian minister and held services in his home near Peever.

In those days, Indians and prairie fires were a constant worry to the pioneers. Many times long lines of Indians with their belongings, led by Chief Gabriel Renville, passed by the Nancarrow home on their way to buy government supplies at Montevideo, Minnesota.

Katherine Malone Waite; Bon Homme, 1880

Her parents and eight of the older children moved from Canada to South Dakota where her father came to help in building the Chicago, Milwaukee and St. Paul Railroad from Yankton to Running Water. Her early life was spent in a log cabin, a double cabin, each section containing two rooms connected by a roofed porch. Their home was surrounded on three sides by Indian tribes including the Santee, Poncas and Yanktons.

Mrs. Waite's father secured a plot of land which adjoined the three Indian reservations. On this plot the Indians met and visited, using this as a common meeting place. Along the Missouri bottoms the Indians buried their dead, burial being made by erecting a scaffold made by setting four posts in the ground and building a platform on them. The body wrapped in his blankets, was placed on this platform, for it was the Indian superstition, that "the spirit wouldn't be released properly under ground." [By Maude Wilson and Dorothee Lyman]

Mable Dora Lee Brownwolf; Ziebach County, 1910

At our new home we have many Indian families for our neighbors. Several of their children go to school with us. Mr. Edward Swan had two girls. Mr. Dick Swan had a boy and a girl. Mr. Oscar Bridwell had two girls and two boys. Then in between there was Mr. Philip Brownwolf, but their children all went to school at Pierre Indian Boarding School. When school was out in the spring there were several young people home from different schools. It was one of these young men who in 1922 became my husband.

That was a queer meeting for two young people. In August or September, I just don't recall, there was a big fair and rodeo going on at Faith, South Dakota. Mr. Brownwolf's family had all gone and left their son, John, home alone. He was going later on horseback. He had been going by our place before and he would stop and talk to all whomever he saw. Well this one time he decided that maybe we could go with him to the fair. He loaded his record player into the buggy drawn by two horses and he came over to Dad, and asked Dad, "Mr. Lee, I would like to trade my record player for your girl." Of course Dad did not approve but after he left I did a lot of coaxing and wanted to go to the fair, so Dad said I could go with the Bridwell girls to the fair, so I went. I came home about four days later, and John bringing me. Dad asked him to take his record player home so it wouldn't get broken. John said, "No, I traded for your girl." So we were married December 29, 1922 in Dupree by Rev. Owens. Avie Langor, Geecy and Thomas Kills First were our witnesses.

Tone Saurer Bamble; Campbell County, 1883

This land was not yet open for settlement, being still a part of the Great Sioux Indian Reservation, so they merely squatted on the "promised land" in June, 1883.

The Sioux Indians were good neighbors and the settlers were not molested, having cultivated their friendship. The Indians came across the Missouri River on the ice and in their canoes to visit and trade with the settlers. Because of honesty and fair dealings they came often to the Bamble home to trade goods and to eat with the family. Many times if food was left on the table after meals they would ask to take it with them, which was gladly given. The Bamble children spent much time playing with Indian children. One was Amos Good Shot who later became a great bronc-buster. In 1888 an Indian Delegation from Standing Rock Agency went to Washington, D. C. Among the 15 who are in the picture of this delegation are: High Eagle – a neighbor who

lived directly across the river from the Bambles; Chief
Grass – whom their post office was later named after.

Helen M. Pettigrew Locke; Moody County, 1873

While yet living in our covered wagon a band of Indians
from the Santee Agency came through with their pack ponies.
They were on the way to the Pipestone Quarry, eighteen
miles east.

Fred Pettigrew invited them into his office and they
sat on the floor in a circle and smoked the "Peace Pipe."

Not long after we came here, while living in the sod
house father traded his horses and harnesses for two yokes
of oxen and an Indian pony. I had no playmates, so after
learning to ride Nellie, the old white pony, I sought out
an Indian girl about my age. Lucy Columbus was her name.
As she couldn't speak my language nor I her's, she would
interest me with beads. She had an older sister who made
moccasins and all kinds of bead work.

Previous to this, C. K. Howard of Sioux Falls, Dakota
Territory, had a Trading Post for the Indians here. The Indians were very friendly and there was a strong tie between
them and the early settlers. There was a Government School
house for the Indians. This was originally a Mission Church.
Before we came the government had taken it over for a
school house and Mr. P. A. Vanice was the teacher for the
Indians. They were still having Sunday Services there when
we came and we often attended. We liked to hear them sing
though we could not understand all they said. The First
Presbyterian Church (Indian) was built in 1874, which is
still in use.

My sister Hattie E., who was about seven years my
senior, was the first teacher for white children. The school
was held in the front room of the Indian schoolhouse. There
was one Indian boy, Charles A. Eastman, who attended.
He said "My father wanted me to go to the white man's
school." He later was sent away to school and later still
a white man became interested to know what could be made
of an Indian, so he sent him to Dartmouth College in the
East. He graduated from there as Dr. Charles A. Eastman.
He also became quite well known as an author.*

Mrs. Helen Pettigrew Locke—1875
Flandreau, Moody County

The nearest railroad at that time was at Marshall, Minnesota, a distance of sixty miles across country. He went with oxen. Some of the Indians with their ox teams went with him. It took a week to make the trip. The first structure was small and soon there was found need for more room, so an addition must be built, then all too soon, another addition.

*For a listing of his books see page 138.

Betsy Himle Swenumson; Yankton County, 1870; Sanborn County, 1880

The Sisseton Reservation had been opened two years before. A building was erected and the store started.

A church was organized and services were held in the store. Rev. Mikelson drove with horse and buggy from Clinton, Minnesota, (fifty miles), to preach to the people. A young Indian, Eddie Skyman, played the organ for the church service. At the first people were afraid of the Indians but they soon learned that the color of skin and hair did not make the person.

Mary Carlson Franzen; Marshall County, 1889

Indians drove past our home in wagons. They usually had many dogs and horses along. They came from western reservations going east to visit the tribes on the Sisseton Reservation. They would stop to water their animals. One time one of the women and a little girl came to the door asking for a loaf of bread. The child noticed a colorful picture on the wall and liked it very much. Mother took it down and gave it to her.

Sometimes white settlers traveled through in covered wagons. One evening mother and we children were home alone when we heard a wagon coming. Mother was afraid when strangers came through when we were alone. She turned the light out and told us to be perfectly quiet. Sometimes they would ask to camp over night on the grassland. Father would give them permission. One time he gave them a watermelon from the garden. They were thankful and we could hear the children's joyful laughter.

Annie Larson; Pennington County, 1885

Annie could speak several languages, Norwegian, Bohemian, besides Indian, as several of her neighbors were Indian.

Gertrude May Preston Maynard; Hand County, 1882

She loved the Indian people and learned from them how to live off from the land using wild grown edibles such as greens, turnips, mushrooms as well as wild plums, cherries, grapes and buffalo berries for jams and jellies to supplement garden foods.

Carol Ralston Rosser; Gregory County, 1897

My parents lived on a homestead near Dirkstown – west of Oacoma, South Dakota, and it was there on September 20, 1897, I was born in a pioneer log house. White people in the area were scarce, therefore, my early playmates were Indian children. One memory remains so vividly of an Indian woman measuring my feet and in a few days she came with a beautiful, handmade beaded pair of moccasins for me.

The family lived for a time at a place on Sully Flats, west of Dixon, South Dakota. Here again, the neighbors were red. What fun we kids did have "not playing Indian" but being Indians! We made and played with our corn husk dolls; picked up a bit of the language, learned to ride the ponies, and were pioneers along with others who lived on the reservation.

PIONEER DAUGHTERS

Amsden, Julia Mattison; Grant County, 1880
Anderson, Cora May; Beadle County, 1883
Anderson, Myrtle Miller; Todd County, 1895
Arbuckle, Catherine Maud Boland; Pennington County, 1879
Armstrong, Kittie Brink; Beadle County, 1882
Ashley, Mina; Charles Mix County, 1885
Astleford, Alice Bauerly; Jones County, 1909
Auld, Agnes Euphemia Ramaga; Aurora, 1882
Aungie, Harriet; Clay County, 1890
Ayer, Lillian Clark; Lawrence County, 1878
Badger, Pearl; Buffalo County, 1871
Baggaley, Jennie Evans; Lawrence County, 1877
Bamble, Tone Saurer; Campbell County, 1883
Bardwell, Mary; Bon Homme County, 1861
Becker, Margaret Heil; Dewey County, 1917
Bennett, Emma F. Ross; Edmunds County, 1883
Berg, Anna Holsten; Butte County, 1886
Berg, Mathilda Andersdotter; Grant County, 1881
Berryman, Anna Wood; Meade County, 1880
Bickelhaupt, Ida Owen; Edmunds County, 1887
Billinghurst, May Bowman; Spink County, 1879
Boesl, Coraline E. Saxton; Bennett County, 1893
Boland, Kate Johnson; Custer County, 1880
Bordeaux, Dorine Smith; Todd County, 1887
Bouzek, Mary Vondra; Hyde County, 1884
Bowles, Martha Ellen Mahaffey; Hand County, 1883
Brakke, Minnie Berge; Moody County, 1876
Brown, Helen A. Smith; Brookings County, 1887
Brownwolf, Mable Dora Lee; Ziebach County, (1910)
Buckley, Nellie; Day County, 1887
Buehler, Selma; Day County, 1887
Buhler, Bertha Geuther; Yankton County, 1878
Cole, Edith; Lawrence County, 1878
Colgrove, Mrs. Samuel; Hamlin County, Lawrence County, 1877

Hanley, Addie Robinson; Pennington County, 1889
Hansen, Ingeborg Iverson; Faulk County, 1888
Hansen, Jette; Brule County, 1874
Harrington, Mrs. Fred; Haakon County, 1890
Henrikson, Bertha; Brookings County, 1877
Herrington, Minnie; Shannon County, 1888
Holmes, Lizzie Elliot; Charles Mix County, 1882
Hood, Mary Roets; Clay County, 1870
Jacobsen, Ethel Collins; Hughes County, 1883
Jenney, Ella; Hutchinson County, 1884
Jensen, Esther Berg; Grant County, 1887
Johnson, Ann Aurilla Mac Daniels; Custer County, 1883
Johnson, Kristina J. Carlson; Hyde County, 1887
Johnson, Philena Everett; Sully County, 1867
Jones, Anna Jorgenson; Turner County, 1884
Jones, Clara Anna Ashman; Hughes County, 1895
Jones, Mae; Edmunds County, 1884
Judson, Mary Jane Horlocker; Meade County, 1868
Keene, Melissa; Clay County, 1870.
Kimball, Clara; Clay County, 1860
King, Iva VanLoon; Marshall County, 1877
Kingman, Emma Nokes; Brule County, 1883
Klebsch, Sarah Ann; Spink County, 1879
Knight, Alice May Nancarrow; Lincoln County, 1874
Krueger, May Green Holmes; Campbell County, 1886
Lang, Ann Harris; Yankton County, 1873
Larson, Annie; Pennington County, 1885
Lathrop, Margaret; Charles Mix County, 1882
Lein, Anna M. Hanson; Brule County, 1883
Locke, Helen M. Pettigrew; Moody County, 1873
Lowe, Amelia Martha Stimson; Clay County, 1873
Lum, McCracken Elshere; Pennington County, 1884
Lumley, Bessie Bagby; Sully County, 1884
Macy, Fanny; Bon Homme County, [1870]
Macy, Jane; Bon Homme County, 1880
Mansfield, Mary Ann; Pennington County, 1883
Martin, Eva; Codington County, 1879
Mathiesen, Ling; Hamlin County, 1881
Maynard, Gertrude May Preston; Hand County, 1882
McDonald, Birdie; Edmunds County, 1885
Mehner, Roxanne Heffelfinger; Brown County, 1883

Tarrant, Mary L.; Meade County, 1895
Tessin, Isabel Hubbell; Day County, 1883
Thomas, Ruth Rebecca Henion; Beadle County, 1884
Thorne, Clara M. Bolster; Minnehaha County, 1872
Traut, Lulu Lee Mooney; Fall River, Hanson and Mc Cook
    Counties, 1884
Trygstad, Kristianna Ortness; Brookings County, 1869
Uhlig, Louise; Lawrence County, 1876
Uken, Clara Lyman; Yankton County, 1888
Uken, Mathilda Aungie; Tripp County, n.d.
Van Camp, Kate; Hyde County, 1883
Van Dyke, Carrie Van Heuvelen; Campbell County, 1886
Van Heuvelen, Jennie Tinholt; Campbell and McPherson Coun-
    ties, 1889
Waldron, Jane Elizabeth; Clay County, 1861
Wallace, Hila Freeman; Fall River County, 1887
Warner, Laura Kentopf; Fall River County, 1904
Weeks, Caroline Stalheim Nelson; Clay County, 1860
Weldin, Mary Jane Gould; Tripp County, 1880
Wertz, Nettie Napes Mitchell; Coddington County, 1878
Westover, Della; Custer County, 1884
White, May Holcomb; Pennington County, 1879
Wilber, Esther Louise Clement; Brown County, 1880
Williamson, Addie Jordan; Sully County, 1883
Williamson, Sarah Van Nuys; Brule County, 1866
Wilson, Ella T.; Aurora County, 1887
Winget, Viola Estella Spry Mumby; Turner and Bon Homme
    Counties, 1883
Woods, Nancy; Butte County, n.d.
Youngquist, Florence De Bell; Todd County, 1885
Zickrick, Ida Mae Potter; Miner County, 1881

BOOKS AND AUTHORS MENTIONED IN TEXT

Anderson, John Alvin. *The Sioux of the Rosebud;* a history in pictures. Photos by John A. Anderson. Text by Henry W. Hamilton and Jean Tyree Hamilton. Norman: University of Oklahoma Press, 1971.

Anderson, Myrtle Miller, *Sioux Memory Gems.* Illustrated by John A. Anderson. [Chicago]: s.n., 1929.

Eastman, Charles Alexander. *From the Deep Woods to Civilization; Chapters in the Autobiography of an Indian.* Lincoln: University of Nebraska Press, 1977.

_____. *The Indian To-day: the past and future of the first American.* Garden City, New York: Doubleday, Page & Co., 1915.

_____. *Indian Scout Talks; a guide for Boys scouts and Campfire girls.* Boston: Little, Brown, and company, 1914.

_____. *Indian boyhood.* New York: McClure, Phillips, and company, 1902.

_____. *Indian Heroes and Great Chieftans.* Boston: Little, Brown, and company, 1910.

_____. *Indian Child Life.* Boston: Little, Brown, and company, 1913.

_____. *Indian Handicrafts.* [S.1.:s.n.] 1905.

_____. *Old Indian Days.* New York: McClure Co., 1907.

_____. *Red Hunters and the Animal People.* New York: Harper & Brothers Publishers, 1904.

_____ and Elaine Goodale Eastman. *Smoky Day's Wigwam Evenings; Indian stories retold.* Boston: Little, Brown, and company, 1910.

_____. *The Souls of the Indian: an interpretation.* Boston: Houghton Mifflin company, [c1911].

_____ and Elaine Goodale Eastman. *Wigwam Evenings: Sioux folk tales retold.* Boston: Little, Brown, and company, [1909].

Standing Bear, Luther. *Land of the Spotted Eagle.* Boston: Houghton Mifflin Company, 1933.

_____. *My Indian Boyhood.* Lincoln: University of Nebraska Press, 1988.

_____. *My People the Sioux.* Edited by E. A. Brininstool. Lincoln: University of Nebraska Press, 1975.